E-Commerce Development with PHP: Build Online Stores from Scratch

A Comprehensive Guide to Building Secure and Scalable E-Commerce Sites

MIGUEL FARMER

RAFAEL SANDERS

All rights reserved

Table of Content

TABLE OF CONTENTS

INTRODUCTION

The world of e-commerce has revolutionized the way businesses interact with customers. The ability to reach a global audience, sell products around the clock, and provide an easy and seamless shopping experience has become a key driver for business success. However, building and managing a successful e-commerce store goes beyond simply creating a website. It involves a comprehensive understanding of various technologies, security measures, customer service practices, marketing strategies, and legal considerations, all of which must work together harmoniously to create a user-friendly and profitable online store.

This book, **E-Commerce Development with PHP: Build Online Stores from Scratch**, is designed to equip you with the knowledge and practical skills needed to create, scale, and maintain a successful e-commerce website using **PHP** and associated technologies. Whether you're a beginner eager to dive into the world of e-commerce development or an experienced developer looking to enhance your skills, this book offers a clear, step-by-step guide to building an e-commerce store from the ground up.

What You Will Learn

Through this book, you will learn the core aspects of **e-commerce development**, starting with basic concepts and progressing to more advanced topics that are essential for running a modern e-commerce business. Each chapter builds upon the previous one, gradually taking you from creating a simple online store to implementing advanced features and preparing your website for launch and growth.

1. **Setting Up Your Development Environment**: You will begin by learning how to set up PHP, MySQL, and Apache for local development, enabling you to start building your store on your local machine before going live.

2. **Building the Core Store Features**: You will walk through the process of creating essential components of your e-commerce store, including user authentication, product catalog, shopping cart functionality, order management, and payment integration.

3. **Optimizing User Experience**: We will guide you in designing a responsive user interface, improving the navigation, and implementing features like search and product filtering. These components are vital to

7

ensuring that customers can find and purchase products with ease.

4. **Handling Complex E-Commerce Features**: As you move into more advanced topics, you will learn how to integrate powerful features such as product recommendations, cross-selling, wishlists, saved carts, and promotional campaigns. These features enhance the shopping experience and drive sales.

5. **Ensuring Security and Compliance**: You will gain a deeper understanding of the legal considerations involved in running an e-commerce site, from data protection regulations like GDPR and CCPA to implementing secure payment gateways and cookie consent pop-ups.

6. **Testing and Debugging**: The book covers essential techniques for testing your PHP code using PHPUnit, debugging common issues, and conducting performance reviews to ensure your site can handle high traffic volumes.

7. **Scaling Your Store for Growth**: Once your store is live, you will learn how to scale it to handle increased traffic, optimize database performance, and ensure that the site remains secure and reliable.

Why PHP?

PHP is a powerful, open-source programming language that has been widely used for web development. It's one of the most popular choices for building dynamic websites, and e-commerce platforms are no exception. With its robust support for databases like MySQL and a vast ecosystem of libraries and frameworks, PHP is an ideal choice for building flexible and scalable e-commerce sites.

PHP allows for:

- **Customizability**: Tailor your e-commerce site to meet your specific business needs.
- **Ease of Use**: PHP is relatively easy to learn for beginners, especially if you already have some experience with programming or web development.
- **Scalability**: PHP's architecture allows for smooth scalability, meaning that as your store grows, you can easily add more features and optimize performance.

Target Audience

This book is designed for a wide range of readers, from absolute beginners to experienced developers:

- **Beginners**: If you're new to PHP or e-commerce development, this book will guide you through the basics, explaining concepts in simple, understandable terms while providing real-world examples and exercises to help solidify your learning.

- **Intermediate Developers**: If you already have some experience with PHP and web development, this book will take you beyond the basics. You will learn how to build a full-fledged e-commerce store, integrate advanced features, and optimize the performance and security of your site.

- **Business Owners and Entrepreneurs**: For business owners who want to create their own e-commerce websites but lack coding experience, this book offers a hands-on guide to creating a store from scratch. The focus on practical applications will help you understand what goes into building a successful e-commerce platform.

A Comprehensive, Practical Guide

Each chapter of this book is carefully structured to provide clear, actionable guidance. The book starts by breaking down the essential components of an e-commerce store and moves into more advanced topics. The chapters are filled with real-world examples, explanations of common best practices, and actionable steps to ensure that you can apply what you've learned to your own projects.

In addition to the core concepts of e-commerce, you will also find practical advice on the following:

- **Optimizing for SEO**: How to ensure your store ranks well in search engines.
- **Legal Considerations**: How to protect customer data and comply with legal regulations.
- **Performance Optimization**: Ensuring your site loads quickly and efficiently even under heavy traffic.
- **User Experience (UX)**: How to design a site that is easy to use, visually appealing, and mobile-friendly.

Preparing for Launch and Post-Launch Maintenance

The final chapters focus on preparing your e-commerce site for launch and ensuring its continued success post-launch. You will learn how to test and debug your website, conduct performance reviews, and implement monitoring and backup systems. You'll also learn how to update and maintain your store after launch, adding new features, improving security, and optimizing for growth.

Conclusion

Building and maintaining a successful e-commerce store is a challenging but rewarding endeavor. With the right tools, knowledge, and strategies, you can create an online store that not only meets the needs of your customers but also scales and evolves with your business.

E-Commerce Development with PHP: Build Online Stores from Scratch is your step-by-step guide to turning your e-commerce vision into reality. Whether you're just getting started or looking to improve an existing store, this book will provide the essential knowledge and skills you need to succeed in the fast-paced world of e-commerce.

Let's get started on building your e-commerce empire!

CHAPTER 1

INTRODUCTION TO E-COMMERCE

Overview of E-Commerce and Its Importance in Today's Market

E-commerce, or electronic commerce, refers to the buying and selling of goods and services over the internet. The rise of the internet and mobile technologies has drastically transformed the way businesses operate, allowing companies to reach customers globally without the need for physical stores. E-commerce has become a vital part of today's economy, with businesses and consumers increasingly opting for the convenience and accessibility of online transactions.

In recent years, e-commerce has seen a rapid surge in adoption. The global shift towards online shopping, accelerated by the pandemic, has established e-commerce as a primary channel for retail. Companies ranging from small startups to large corporations are leveraging e-commerce platforms to offer products and services to a wider audience, streamline operations, and reduce costs. For consumers, online shopping offers flexibility, convenience, and competitive pricing, making it a preferred method for purchasing products.

The importance of e-commerce is reflected in statistics: global e-commerce sales are expected to surpass $6 trillion by 2024, and this figure continues to grow. As businesses adapt to changing consumer behavior, e-commerce provides the necessary tools to reach and engage customers, offering both new opportunities and challenges in an increasingly digital world.

Key Concepts and Types of E-Commerce Businesses (B2B, B2C, etc.)

There are several different models of e-commerce, each serving distinct market needs. Understanding these models is crucial for building a successful e-commerce platform. The key types include:

1. **Business to Consumer (B2C)**: This is the most common and widely recognized e-commerce model. B2C involves transactions between businesses and individual customers. Examples include online retailers like Amazon, eBay, and small businesses that sell products directly to consumers. B2C is often associated with e-commerce sites that offer a wide range of consumer goods, such as electronics, clothing, and groceries.

2. **Business to Business (B2B)**: In the B2B model, businesses sell products or services to other businesses. Transactions in this category often involve wholesale products, industrial equipment, and services such as

software solutions. For instance, a company that manufactures office supplies may sell products in bulk to retailers or corporations. B2B platforms tend to have a longer sales cycle and require more complex systems for managing bulk orders, contracts, and negotiations.

3. **Consumer to Consumer (C2C)**: C2C platforms allow consumers to sell goods and services directly to other consumers. Examples of C2C platforms include eBay, Craigslist, and Poshmark. These platforms typically act as intermediaries, providing the tools and infrastructure for consumers to buy and sell items. C2C e-commerce has grown alongside the popularity of peer-to-peer transactions, especially in second-hand goods markets.

4. **Consumer to Business (C2B)**: C2B is a less common model but involves individuals offering products or services to businesses. A typical example could be a freelance graphic designer offering services to companies or a photographer selling stock photos to marketing agencies. This model is often seen in the gig economy and creative industries.

5. **Business to Government (B2G)**: B2G involves businesses providing goods or services to government agencies. While not as common in consumer-facing businesses, B2G transactions can involve contracts for infrastructure, services, or technology. E-government

platforms, such as public procurement portals, fall under this category.

Each of these models has unique requirements and challenges. Understanding which type of e-commerce your project will fall under is key to building the right platform and ensuring that it meets the needs of both the business and its customers.

Why PHP is a Great Choice for Building E-Commerce Sites

PHP (Hypertext Preprocessor) has been a popular programming language for web development for decades. When it comes to building e-commerce sites, PHP stands out for several reasons:

1. **Open Source and Cost-Effective**: PHP is an open-source language, meaning it's free to use and has a large, active community contributing to its development. This reduces costs for businesses looking to develop e-commerce websites, as they don't need to pay for proprietary software licenses.

2. **Flexibility and Customization**: PHP offers excellent flexibility and scalability, allowing developers to customize e-commerce platforms based on specific business needs. Whether you're building a simple online store or a complex marketplace with hundreds of thousands of products, PHP can be adapted to suit your requirements.

3. **Wide Range of E-Commerce Frameworks**: PHP is home to many powerful frameworks and platforms designed specifically for building e-commerce sites. Popular tools like WooCommerce (for WordPress), Magento, and PrestaShop offer ready-made solutions that can be easily customized and extended.

4. **Strong Database Integration**: PHP works seamlessly with MySQL, the most commonly used relational database management system for e-commerce sites. The combination of PHP and MySQL is highly efficient for handling product catalogs, inventory management, orders, and customer data.

5. **Security Features**: PHP provides built-in functions for securing sensitive data, such as user passwords and transaction details. Features like password hashing, data sanitization, and secure session management make PHP a secure choice for handling online payments and customer information.

6. **Wide Hosting Support**: PHP is supported by virtually every hosting provider, making it easy and affordable to find reliable web hosting for your e-commerce site. Additionally, most hosting services offer specific support for PHP-based applications, ensuring smooth deployment.

7. **Large Community and Resources**: PHP has a vast community of developers who contribute to forums,

tutorials, and libraries, offering extensive resources for problem-solving and learning. This community support makes it easier to find solutions to common challenges in e-commerce development.

Basic Requirements and Tools for Starting an E-Commerce Project

To start building an e-commerce site, you need to gather both the technical and business components. Here are the basic requirements and tools that you'll need:

1. **Domain Name and Hosting**:
   o Choose a domain name that is relevant to your business and easy to remember.
   o Select a hosting provider that supports PHP and MySQL. Shared hosting may be suitable for smaller stores, but larger stores may require VPS or dedicated hosting.
2. **Development Tools**:
   o **Text Editor/IDE**: Tools like Visual Studio Code, Sublime Text, or PHPStorm are excellent for writing PHP code. These editors offer syntax highlighting, debugging tools, and extensions that improve productivity.
   o **Version Control**: Use Git for version control to manage your project's codebase. GitHub, GitLab,

and Bitbucket are popular platforms for collaborating and storing your code.

- o **Database Management**: phpMyAdmin is a popular tool for managing MySQL databases through a web interface. Alternatively, MySQL Workbench offers a more powerful graphical interface.

3. **PHP Framework or CMS**:
   - o For beginners or those seeking a quicker development cycle, using a CMS like WordPress (with WooCommerce) or an e-commerce platform like PrestaShop is a good choice.
   - o For more advanced users, building from scratch with a PHP framework like Laravel or Symfony allows for greater control and customization.

4. **Design and User Experience (UX)**:
   - o Use CSS frameworks like Bootstrap for responsive design and to ensure that your e-commerce site works well across all devices.
   - o Tools like Figma or Adobe XD can help you design a user-friendly interface and plan the overall layout of your store.

5. **Payment Gateway Integration**:
   - o Choose payment gateways like PayPal, Stripe, or Authorize.Net to process payments securely.

- o Ensure you integrate these gateways using their provided APIs for smooth and secure transactions.

6. **Security**:
   - o Implement SSL certificates for secure data transmission.
   - o Use PHP's built-in functions to secure user data, such as password hashing and data sanitization.

By the end of this chapter, readers should have a solid understanding of what e-commerce is, the different types of e-commerce businesses, and why PHP is an ideal language for building secure, scalable e-commerce sites. The basic requirements and tools discussed will set the foundation for the development process, ensuring that readers are equipped to start building their e-commerce sites from scratch.

CHAPTER 2

SETTING UP YOUR DEVELOPMENT ENVIRONMENT

Installing PHP, MySQL, and Apache for Local Development

Before you can start building your e-commerce site with PHP, you need to set up your local development environment. This environment will allow you to run and test your PHP code, interact with a MySQL database, and simulate a web server, all from your local machine.

1. **Installing PHP**: PHP is a server-side scripting language that processes and generates dynamic content for your website. To install PHP, you'll need to download the latest stable version from the official PHP website. However, manually installing PHP can be complicated, so it's recommended to use a preconfigured package like XAMPP (which includes PHP, MySQL, and Apache).

2. **Installing MySQL**: MySQL is a popular relational database management system (RDBMS) used to store and manage your e-commerce data (such as product listings, orders, and customer information). Like PHP, MySQL can be installed manually, but it's easier to install it as part

of a package (such as XAMPP or WAMP) to simplify setup.

3. **Installing Apache Web Server**: Apache is a widely used open-source web server software. It serves PHP files and delivers them to users' browsers. Apache runs as a service on your local machine during development, allowing you to preview your e-commerce site in real time. You can install Apache manually, but like PHP and MySQL, it's easier to use a package like XAMPP or WAMP, which will install and configure Apache automatically.

By installing these components on your machine, you'll be able to run a complete local server environment, including PHP processing, database management, and content delivery through Apache.

Introduction to Web Servers and Databases

1. **Web Servers**: A web server is responsible for accepting requests from users (usually through a web browser), processing those requests, and delivering content back to the user. When you're building a dynamic e-commerce site, a web server like Apache will handle the requests for PHP files, execute the PHP code, and return the generated HTML to the user's browser.

22

Web servers are essential because they bridge the gap between the server-side (where your code and database are hosted) and the client-side (the user's browser). Apache is one of the most popular open-source web servers and is often paired with PHP to create a powerful, flexible environment for web development.

2. **Databases**: A database stores all of the dynamic content for your website, such as user information, product listings, orders, and payments. MySQL is one of the most widely used relational database management systems (RDBMS), and it works seamlessly with PHP.

   In MySQL, data is stored in tables, which are organized into rows and columns. Each table is related to other tables through keys (primary keys and foreign keys). For example, the products table may have a foreign key that links each product to a specific category in a categories table. As an e-commerce site grows, efficient database management becomes crucial for storing and retrieving large amounts of data.

Using XAMPP and Other Local Development Environments

For most beginners, setting up a development environment using individual software installations (PHP, Apache, MySQL) can be complex and time-consuming. Instead, you can use integrated development environments (IDEs) or software packages like XAMPP, which bundle everything you need into one package.

1. **XAMPP**: XAMPP is a free, open-source software package that includes PHP, MySQL, and Apache, and it is one of the easiest ways to set up a local development environment for PHP-based projects. XAMPP automatically configures Apache and MySQL, so you don't have to worry about manually setting up each component.

   To install XAMPP:

   o Download the XAMPP installer from the official website.
   o Follow the installation prompts to install XAMPP on your machine.
   o After installation, open the XAMPP control panel to start the Apache server and MySQL database server.
   o Once both services are running, you can access your local PHP files by navigating to `localhost` in your browser.

   XAMPP provides an easy-to-use dashboard, allowing you to manage and control the services running on your local server. It also includes phpMyAdmin, a graphical interface for managing your MySQL databases.

2. **Other Local Development Environments**: While XAMPP is one of the most popular options, there are other local development environments that you can use to set up your PHP, MySQL, and Apache stack:

   o **MAMP**: A similar package to XAMPP, MAMP offers a user-friendly interface for macOS and Windows. It provides PHP, MySQL, and Apache in one installation.

   o **WAMP**: WAMP is another option for Windows users, providing a similar stack as XAMPP, including Apache, MySQL, and PHP.

   o **Laragon**: A lightweight and fast local development environment that's especially popular for Laravel and PHP development. Laragon supports Apache, MySQL, PHP, and more.

These alternatives work similarly to XAMPP, providing a complete local environment for web development without the hassle of configuring each component individually.

Overview of IDEs and Tools for PHP Development

When working with PHP, a good IDE (Integrated Development Environment) or text editor can significantly improve productivity by providing features like syntax highlighting, error checking, debugging tools, and code completion. Here are some popular tools for PHP development:

1. **PHPStorm**: PHPStorm is a powerful and feature-rich IDE specifically designed for PHP developers. It provides advanced features such as intelligent code completion, error detection, version control integration, and debugging tools. PHPStorm is ideal for professional developers working on large-scale projects but comes with a paid license.

2. **Visual Studio Code (VS Code)**: Visual Studio Code is a free, open-source text editor that's highly customizable and supports PHP development through extensions. While it's not an IDE in the traditional sense, it offers features like syntax highlighting, integrated terminal, debugging, and extensions for version control and PHP development. It's lightweight and popular among developers.

3. **Sublime Text**: Sublime Text is a fast and simple text editor with great support for PHP development. It features syntax highlighting, split editing, and a robust package ecosystem. Sublime Text is lightweight and ideal for

smaller projects, but it may lack some advanced debugging features compared to PHPStorm.

4. **Atom**: Atom is another free, open-source text editor that can be customized for PHP development. Like VS Code, it relies on packages and plugins for PHP support. Atom has a friendly interface and is great for developers who prefer a more flexible editor.

5. **NetBeans**: NetBeans is an open-source IDE that supports multiple programming languages, including PHP. It provides features like code completion, debugging, and a built-in server for testing PHP applications. While not as popular as PHPStorm, it's still a solid option for PHP developers.

6. **Brackets**: Brackets is a free, open-source text editor designed for web development, and it supports PHP through plugins. It's particularly useful for front-end development but can be extended for PHP back-end development as well.

7. **Version Control Tools (Git)**: Version control is essential when working on any development project, including e-commerce sites. Git allows you to track changes to your codebase, collaborate with other developers, and manage different versions of your project. GitHub, GitLab, and Bitbucket are popular platforms that offer hosting for Git repositories, making it easy to manage your project's code.

By the end of this chapter, readers should be familiar with how to set up a local development environment for PHP and MySQL using tools like XAMPP, MAMP, or WAMP. Additionally, they will understand the role of web servers and databases in web development and how to choose the right IDE or text editor for PHP development. This foundation is crucial for building and testing their e-commerce sites locally before deploying them to production servers.

CHAPTER 3

UNDERSTANDING THE BASICS OF PHP AND MYSQL

PHP Syntax and Basic Constructs (Variables, Loops, Conditionals)

PHP is a server-side scripting language designed for web development. It can be embedded directly into HTML and is often used to create dynamic and interactive web pages. In this section, we'll cover the fundamental PHP syntax, along with some basic constructs such as variables, loops, and conditionals that form the backbone of PHP programming.

1. **PHP Syntax**:
   - **PHP Tags**: PHP code is written inside `<?php` and `?>` tags. Anything outside of these tags is treated as regular HTML.

   php

   ```
   <?php
     echo "Hello, world!";
   ?>
   ```

- o **Comments**: Comments can be added to explain code. Single-line comments start with //, while multi-line comments are wrapped in /* and */.

```php
// This is a single-line comment
/* This is a
    multi-line comment */
```

2. **Variables**: Variables in PHP are denoted by a dollar sign ($) followed by the variable name. PHP variables don't need to be declared before they are used, and their type is determined dynamically at runtime.

```php
$name = "John Doe";
$age = 30;
```

- o **Variable Types**: PHP supports a variety of data types such as integers, strings, floats, arrays, and objects.
- o **Concatenation**: You can combine strings using the dot (.) operator.

```php
echo "Hello, " . $name;
```

3. **Loops**: Loops are used to repeat code multiple times. PHP supports several loop structures:

   o **For Loop**: Typically used when you know how many times the loop should run.

   php

   ```php
   for ($i = 0; $i < 5; $i++) {
     echo $i . "<br>";
   }
   ```

   o **While Loop**: Used when you don't know how many times the loop will run, but you want it to continue as long as a condition is true.

   php

   ```php
   $i = 0;
   while ($i < 5) {
     echo $i . "<br>";
     $i++;
   }
   ```

   o **Foreach Loop**: Particularly useful for iterating over arrays.

   php

```
$fruits    =    ["apple",    "banana",
"cherry"];
foreach ($fruits as $fruit) {
   echo $fruit . "<br>";
}
```

4. **Conditionals**: Conditional statements allow you to execute different code based on whether a condition is true or false.

    o **If Statement**: Executes code if the condition is true.

    php

    ```
    if ($age > 18) {
       echo "You are an adult.";
    }
    ```

    o **Else Statement**: Executes code if the condition is false.

    php

    ```
    if ($age > 18) {
       echo "You are an adult.";
    } else {
       echo "You are a minor.";
    }
    ```

o **Switch Statement**: A cleaner way to handle multiple conditions.

```php
php

switch ($day) {
  case "Monday":
    echo "Start of the week!";
    break;
  case "Friday":
    echo "End of the week!";
    break;
  default:
    echo "Have a good day!";
}
```

Introduction to MySQL Databases and SQL Queries

1. **MySQL Databases**: MySQL is a relational database management system (RDBMS) used to store and manage data. In a MySQL database, data is stored in tables, which consist of rows and columns. Each table typically represents an entity (e.g., customers, products, orders) and its properties.

    o **Database Structure**: A database may contain multiple tables. Each table is made up of fields (columns) and records (rows). Each record represents an entry, such as a customer or a product.

33

o **Primary Keys**: Each table should have a primary key, which uniquely identifies each row in the table (e.g., `product_id`, `user_id`).

o **Foreign Keys**: Foreign keys are used to create relationships between tables. For example, an `orders` table might have a foreign key linking to the `customers` table, showing which customer placed the order.

2. **SQL Queries**: SQL (Structured Query Language) is used to interact with a MySQL database. You can use SQL to retrieve, insert, update, and delete data in the database. Below are some basic SQL queries:

   o **SELECT**: Used to retrieve data from one or more tables.

   ```sql
   SELECT * FROM products;
   ```

   o **WHERE**: Used to filter records based on a condition.

   ```sql
   SELECT * FROM products WHERE category = 'Electronics';
   ```

   o **INSERT**: Used to insert new data into a table.

34

```
sql
```

```sql
INSERT INTO products (name, price,
category) VALUES ('Laptop', 899.99,
'Electronics');
```

- o **UPDATE**: Used to modify existing data.

```
sql
```

```sql
UPDATE products SET price = 799.99
WHERE name = 'Laptop';
```

- o **DELETE**: Used to delete data from a table.

```
sql
```

```sql
DELETE FROM products WHERE name =
'Laptop';
```

- o **JOIN**: Used to combine data from two or more tables based on a related column.

```
sql
```

```sql
SELECT              orders.order_id,
customers.name FROM orders
JOIN customers ON orders.customer_id
= customers.customer_id;
```

3. **Database Relationships**:

   o **One-to-Many**: One record in one table is related to multiple records in another table (e.g., one customer can place many orders).

   o **Many-to-Many**: Multiple records in one table are related to multiple records in another table (e.g., products and categories).

How PHP Interacts with MySQL for Dynamic Content

PHP and MySQL work together to build dynamic websites. PHP scripts interact with MySQL databases to retrieve, store, and display data on a website. This enables websites to show up-to-date information (such as product listings, order details, or user profiles) without needing to manually update the content.

1. **Connecting PHP to MySQL**: To interact with a MySQL database from PHP, you first need to establish a connection. This can be done using PHP's mysqli or PDO extensions. Below is an example of how to connect to MySQL using mysqli.

```php
$servername = "localhost";
$username = "root";
$password = "";
$dbname = "ecommerce";
```

```php
// Create connection
$conn = new mysqli($servername, $username,
$password, $dbname);

// Check connection
if ($conn->connect_error) {
  die("Connection   failed:   "   .   $conn-
>connect_error);
}
```

2. **Retrieving Data from MySQL**: Once the connection is established, you can run SQL queries from PHP to retrieve data from the database. Here's an example of how to fetch product details from a `products` table.

php

```php
$sql   =   "SELECT   id,   name,   price   FROM
products";
$result = $conn->query($sql);

if ($result->num_rows > 0) {
  while($row = $result->fetch_assoc()) {
    echo "Product: " . $row["name"] . " -
Price: " . $row["price"] . "<br>";
  }
} else {
  echo "0 results";
```

```
}
```

3. **Inserting Data into MySQL**: You can also insert data into the database using PHP. For example, if a user adds a product to the cart, you can insert the data into an orders table.

php

```
$sql = "INSERT INTO orders (user_id,
product_id, quantity)
VALUES (1, 2, 3)";

if ($conn->query($sql) === TRUE) {
  echo "New record created successfully";
} else {
  echo "Error: " . $sql . "<br>" . $conn-
>error;
}
```

4. **Using Prepared Statements**: Prepared statements are important for security, especially when accepting user input. They help prevent SQL injection attacks by separating SQL code from user input.

php

```
$stmt = $conn->prepare("INSERT INTO
products (name, price, category) VALUES (?,
?, ?)");
$stmt->bind_param("sss", $name, $price,
$category);

$name = "Smartphone";
$price = "599.99";
$category = "Electronics";
$stmt->execute();
```

5. **Closing the Connection**: Always close the database connection after you're done interacting with the database.

```
php
```

```
$conn->close();
```

By the end of this chapter, readers will have a foundational understanding of PHP syntax and basic constructs, how to interact with MySQL databases, and how PHP can be used to dynamically fetch and display content from a MySQL database. This knowledge is essential for creating a dynamic, data-driven e-commerce website.

CHAPTER 4

BUILDING A BASIC E-COMMERCE STORE FRAMEWORK

Planning Your Online Store Architecture

Before you dive into coding your e-commerce store, it's crucial to plan the architecture. Proper planning ensures scalability, maintainability, and security of your site as it grows. In this section, we'll discuss the key components you need to consider when planning your online store architecture.

1. **Identify Core Features**: Every e-commerce store shares certain core features that are necessary for it to function. These features include:
   - o **Product Catalog**: A system to display products with details like images, descriptions, and prices.
   - o **Shopping Cart**: A cart where users can add and remove items before proceeding to checkout.
   - o **User Accounts**: A system for customers to create accounts, log in, and track their orders.
   - o **Checkout and Payment**: A secure checkout system that processes customer orders and payments.

- o **Order Management**: A system for admins to manage customer orders and update their statuses (e.g., shipped, pending).
- o **Admin Panel**: An interface for the store owner or admin to manage products, orders, and users.

2. **Database Structure and Relationships**: The architecture should include a well-structured database to store products, user information, orders, and other data. A typical e-commerce database might include tables for:

- o **Users**: Stores customer details (e.g., name, email, password, address).
- o **Products**: Stores product details (e.g., name, description, price, stock quantity).
- o **Orders**: Tracks customer orders (e.g., user_id, product_id, quantity, total price).
- o **Categories**: Organizes products into categories for easier browsing.
- o **Shopping Cart**: Stores cart items temporarily for each user.

Example relationships:

- o **One-to-Many**: One user can have many orders.
- o **Many-to-Many**: A product can belong to multiple categories, and a category can contain multiple products.

3. **User Interface (UI)**: The UI of the store should be user-friendly, responsive (working across devices), and visually appealing. The design should make it easy for customers to navigate the site, find products, add items to the cart, and complete purchases.

4. **Security Considerations**:
   o **Encryption**: Sensitive data such as passwords and payment information should always be encrypted.
   o **SSL/TLS**: Secure the site with SSL certificates to protect customer information during transactions.
   o **Input Validation**: Ensure all data input from users (e.g., form submissions, search queries) is properly sanitized to prevent SQL injection and other attacks.

Creating the Basic File Structure for Your Store

A clean and organized file structure is essential for maintaining the store. Here's a basic file structure for an e-commerce store using PHP and MySQL:

```bash
/ecommerce-store
    /assets
        /css
        /images
```

```
/js
/config
    db.php
    config.php
/includes
    header.php
    footer.php
    nav.php
/admin
    index.php
    manage-products.php
    manage-orders.php
/cart
    cart.php
    checkout.php
/products
    index.php
    details.php
/users
    login.php
    register.php
    profile.php
/orders
    view-order.php
    order-status.php
/templates
    product-listing.php
    order-summary.php
/uploads
```

```
(for product images)
index.php
```

- **/assets**: Contains static files like CSS for styling, JavaScript for functionality, and images (e.g., product images).
- **/config**: Holds configuration files such as database connection settings (db.php) and general site settings (config.php).
- **/includes**: Contains reusable components like headers, footers, and navigation menus.
- **/admin**: Admin pages to manage products, orders, and users.
- **/cart**: Handles the shopping cart and checkout process.
- **/products**: Displays products and their details.
- **/users**: Manages user login, registration, and profiles.
- **/orders**: Tracks orders and their status.
- **/templates**: Houses templates for product listings, order summaries, etc.
- **/uploads**: Stores images uploaded by users or administrators, such as product images.

Building a Simple Product Catalog with PHP and MySQL

Now that you've planned the architecture and organized the file structure, it's time to start building the basic functionality of your e-commerce store. One of the first things we'll build is the

product catalog, where users can view available products. Let's go step by step.

1. **Database Setup**: First, create a MySQL database and a table for storing products. Here's an example of how to set up a basic `products` table:

sql

```sql
CREATE TABLE products (
    product_id INT AUTO_INCREMENT PRIMARY KEY,
    name VARCHAR(255) NOT NULL,
    description TEXT,
    price DECIMAL(10, 2) NOT NULL,
    stock_quantity INT NOT NULL,
    image VARCHAR(255),
    created_at      TIMESTAMP      DEFAULT CURRENT_TIMESTAMP
);
```

   o `product_id`: A unique identifier for each product.

   o `name`: The product name.

   o `description`: A detailed description of the product.

   o `price`: The price of the product.

45

o stock_quantity: The available stock for the product.

o image: The URL to the product image (this could be a file path or URL).

o created_at: A timestamp for when the product was added.

2. **Product Catalog Page**: Create a page where users can view all the products. Here's an example of how you might query the database and display the products using PHP.

File: /products/index.php:

php

```php
<?php
include '../config/db.php';    // Database connection

// Query to get all products
$sql = "SELECT * FROM products";
$result = $conn->query($sql);

if ($result->num_rows > 0) {
    while($row = $result->fetch_assoc()) {
        echo "<div class='product'>";
```

```php
        echo  "<img  src='../uploads/"  .
$row['image'] . "' alt='" . $row['name'] .
"'>";
        echo  "<h3>"  .  $row['name']  .
"</h3>";
        echo "<p>" . $row['description'] .
"</p>";
        echo "<p>Price: $" . $row['price']
. "</p>";
        echo  "<a  href='details.php?id="  .
$row['product_id'] . "'>View Details</a>";
        echo "</div>";
    }
} else {
    echo "No products found.";
}
?>
```

- o **Database Connection**: We include the db.php file to establish a connection to the MySQL database.

- o **Query**: We use a simple SQL query to fetch all products from the products table.

- o **Displaying Data**: We loop through the result set and display the product name, description, price, and an image (if available). We also provide a link to a product details page (details.php).

47

3. **Displaying Product Details**: To display detailed information for each product, we create a product details page. This page will show a single product's full details, such as name, description, price, and image.

File: /products/details.php:

php

```php
<?php
include '../config/db.php';   // Database
connection

// Get the product ID from the URL
$product_id = $_GET['id'];

// Query to get the specific product
$sql = "SELECT * FROM products WHERE
product_id = $product_id";
$result = $conn->query($sql);

if ($result->num_rows > 0) {
    $row = $result->fetch_assoc();
    echo "<div class='product-details'>";
    echo    "<img    src='../uploads/"    .
$row['image'] . "' alt='" . $row['name'] .
"'>";
    echo "<h3>" . $row['name'] . "</h3>";
```

```
    echo   "<p>"   .   $row['description']   .
"</p>";
    echo "<p>Price: $" . $row['price']   .
"</p>";
    echo            "<p>Stock:       "          .
$row['stock_quantity'] . "</p>";
    echo "<button>Add to Cart</button>";
    echo "</div>";
} else {
    echo "Product not found.";
}
?>
```

- o **Getting the Product ID**: We retrieve the product ID from the URL (using $_GET['id']).
- o **Query**: We query the database for the product with the specific product_id.
- o **Displaying Product Details**: We display the product's image, name, description, price, and stock quantity.

By the end of this chapter, you will have a basic e-commerce store framework with a product catalog where users can view a list of products and see detailed information about each one. You will also have learned how to set up the database, structure your project files, and connect PHP with MySQL to fetch and display dynamic content.

CHAPTER 5

DESIGNING THE DATABASE SCHEMA

In this chapter, we'll focus on designing the database schema for your e-commerce store. A well-designed database schema is essential for storing and retrieving data efficiently, ensuring the site scales as it grows, and maintaining data integrity. We'll go through the process of creating tables for products, users, and orders, discuss the importance of foreign keys and normalization for scalability, and implement relationships between tables to support the core functionality of an e-commerce store.

Creating Tables for Products, Users, and Orders

To build an effective database schema, we need to identify the core entities of your e-commerce store and create tables to store relevant data. The main entities for our store are **products**, **users**, and **orders**. Each of these entities will have its own table in the database.

1. **Creating the Users Table**: The `users` table stores information about customers and admins who can log into the system. This table includes essential user details like name, email, password, and address.

sql

```sql
CREATE TABLE users (
    user_id  INT  AUTO_INCREMENT  PRIMARY
KEY,
    first_name VARCHAR(100) NOT NULL,
    last_name VARCHAR(100) NOT NULL,
    email VARCHAR(255) UNIQUE NOT NULL,
    password VARCHAR(255) NOT NULL,
    address TEXT,
    phone_number VARCHAR(15),
    role ENUM('customer', 'admin') DEFAULT
'customer',
    created_at       TIMESTAMP       DEFAULT
CURRENT_TIMESTAMP
);
```

- o user_id: A unique identifier for each user.
- o first_name and last_name: User's personal information.
- o email: The user's email (unique to avoid duplicates).
- o password: A hashed password for secure authentication.
- o address: The user's shipping address.
- o phone_number: The user's phone number (optional).

52

o role: Defines the user role, either customer or admin.

o created_at: Timestamp when the account was created.

2. **Creating the Products Table**: The products table stores details about the products that are available for sale in the store. This includes the product name, description, price, stock quantity, and image.

sql

```sql
CREATE TABLE products (
    product_id INT AUTO_INCREMENT PRIMARY
KEY,
    name VARCHAR(255) NOT NULL,
    description TEXT,
    price DECIMAL(10, 2) NOT NULL,
    stock_quantity INT NOT NULL,
    image VARCHAR(255),
    category_id INT,
    created_at        TIMESTAMP        DEFAULT
CURRENT_TIMESTAMP,
    FOREIGN KEY (category_id) REFERENCES
categories(category_id)
);
```

o product_id: A unique identifier for each product.

53

- o `name`: The name of the product.
- o `description`: A detailed description of the product.
- o `price`: The price of the product.
- o `stock_quantity`: The available quantity of the product in stock.
- o `image`: A URL or file path to the product image.
- o `category_id`: A foreign key linking the product to a category (we'll create a `categories` table for this).
- o `created_at`: Timestamp for when the product was added.

3. **Creating the Orders Table**: The `orders` table tracks customer orders. Each order belongs to a user and can contain multiple products. We will store the order date, the total price, and the user who placed the order.

sql

```
CREATE TABLE orders (
    order_id INT AUTO_INCREMENT PRIMARY
KEY,
    user_id INT NOT NULL,
    total_price DECIMAL(10, 2) NOT NULL,
    order_status          ENUM('pending',
'shipped',    'delivered',    'cancelled')
DEFAULT 'pending',
```

```
    order_date       TIMESTAMP       DEFAULT
CURRENT_TIMESTAMP,
    FOREIGN   KEY   (user_id)   REFERENCES
users(user_id)
);
```

- o order_id: A unique identifier for each order.
- o user_id: A foreign key linking the order to the user who placed it.
- o total_price: The total cost of the order.
- o order_status: The current status of the order (e.g., pending, shipped, delivered, or cancelled).
- o order_date: Timestamp of when the order was placed.

4. **Creating the Order Details Table**: Since each order can contain multiple products, we need a separate table to store the details of each product in the order (e.g., product ID, quantity, and price). This is a **many-to-many** relationship between orders and products.

sql

```sql
CREATE TABLE order_details (
    order_detail_id   INT   AUTO_INCREMENT
PRIMARY KEY,
    order_id INT NOT NULL,
    product_id INT NOT NULL,
    quantity INT NOT NULL,
```

```
price DECIMAL(10, 2) NOT NULL,
FOREIGN   KEY   (order_id)   REFERENCES
orders(order_id),
FOREIGN   KEY   (product_id)   REFERENCES
products(product_id)
);
```

- o `order_detail_id`: A unique identifier for each order detail.
- o `order_id`: A foreign key linking to the `orders` table.
- o `product_id`: A foreign key linking to the `products` table.
- o `quantity`: The quantity of the product in the order.
- o `price`: The price of the product at the time of the order.

Using Foreign Keys and Normalization for Scalability

1. **Foreign Keys**: Foreign keys are used to maintain relationships between different tables. In the example above:
   - o The `category_id` in the `products` table references the `category_id` in the `categories` table (we'll discuss this table in a moment).

o The user_id in the orders table references the user_id in the users table.

o The order_id in the order_details table references the order_id in the orders table, and product_id references product_id in the products table.

By using foreign keys, we ensure that data in one table (e.g., products) is consistent with related data in other tables (e.g., orders), which helps maintain data integrity. For example, an order cannot exist without a valid user, and each product must exist in the product catalog.

2. **Normalization**: Database normalization is the process of organizing data to reduce redundancy and improve efficiency. We apply normalization by breaking the data into smaller, related tables and ensuring that each piece of data is stored only once.

   o **First Normal Form (1NF)**: Ensures that each column contains atomic (indivisible) values. For example, the address column in the users table contains a single address, not a list of addresses.

   o **Second Normal Form (2NF)**: Ensures that all non-key attributes are fully dependent on the primary key. For instance, the order_details table contains the `product_id`, `order_id`, and other attributes related to the order.

o **Third Normal Form (3NF)**: Ensures that there are no transitive dependencies, i.e., non-key attributes should not depend on other non-key attributes.

By following these rules, you can design a scalable and efficient database that can handle large amounts of data.

Implementing Relationships Between Tables (One-to-Many, Many-to-Many)

1. **One-to-Many Relationship**: A **one-to-many** relationship occurs when one record in a table is associated with multiple records in another table. For example, one user can have multiple orders, but each order belongs to only one user. In our schema:
   o The `users` table has a **one-to-many** relationship with the `orders` table. This is represented by the `user_id` foreign key in the `orders` table, linking each order to a specific user.

2. **Many-to-Many Relationship**: A **many-to-many** relationship occurs when multiple records in one table are associated with multiple records in another table. For example, a product can appear in many orders, and each order can contain many products. In our schema:

- o The orders table and the products table have a **many-to-many** relationship. We implement this relationship using the order_details table, which holds the many-to-many associations between orders and products, with columns for order_id, product_id, quantity, and price.

Conclusion

By the end of this chapter, you should have a solid understanding of how to design a relational database schema for an e-commerce store. You learned how to create tables for products, users, and orders, apply foreign keys to enforce relationships, and normalize the database to ensure scalability and data integrity. This database schema will serve as the foundation for building the dynamic features of your e-commerce store, such as product catalogs, user accounts, and order management.

CHAPTER 6

USER AUTHENTICATION AND MANAGEMENT

In this chapter, we'll focus on building a user authentication system for your e-commerce store. A robust authentication system ensures that users can securely log in, access their accounts, and interact with the store. We'll cover how to build a login system using PHP and MySQL, create user roles such as admin and customer, and implement password hashing to ensure secure authentication.

Building a Login System with PHP and MySQL

To allow users to log into your e-commerce store, you'll need to create a secure login system. The system will authenticate users based on their credentials (email and password) stored in the database.

1. **Creating the Login Form**: First, create a login form that allows users to input their email and password. This form will be displayed to users when they visit the login page.

   File: /users/login.php:

php

```php
<?php
session_start(); // Start the session to
store user login state
if (isset($_SESSION['user_id'])) {
    // Redirect logged-in users to the home
page
    header("Location: home.php");
    exit();
}
?>

<form method="POST" action="login.php">
    <label for="email">Email:</label>
    <input      type="email"     id="email"
name="email" required>
    <label
for="password">Password:</label>
    <input  type="password"  id="password"
name="password" required>
    <button                  type="submit"
name="login">Login</button>
</form>

<?php
if (isset($_POST['login'])) {
    // Handle login request
    $email = $_POST['email'];
```

```php
$password = $_POST['password'];

include '../config/db.php'; // Include
the database connection

// Query to check if the email exists
in the database
$sql = "SELECT * FROM users WHERE email
= ?";
$stmt = $conn->prepare($sql);
$stmt->bind_param("s", $email);
$stmt->execute();
$result = $stmt->get_result();

if ($result->num_rows > 0) {
    $user = $result->fetch_assoc();
    // Verify the password using
password_verify
    if (password_verify($password,
$user['password'])) {
        // Password is correct, start
the session and set session variables
        $_SESSION['user_id']        =
$user['user_id'];
        $_SESSION['user_email']     =
$user['email'];
        $_SESSION['user_role']      =
$user['role']; // Store user role
```

```
                    // Redirect the user based on
their role
            if ($user['role'] == 'admin')
{
                header("Location:
admin/index.php");
            } else {
                header("Location:
home.php");
            }
            exit();
        } else {
            echo "Incorrect password.";
        }
    } else {
        echo "User not found.";
    }
}
?>
```

- o **Form Handling**: The form submits the email and password to the `login.php` script via the `POST` method.
- o **Database Query**: The script checks if the email exists in the `users` table. If it does, it retrieves the user's information.
- o **Password Verification**: The `password_verify` function is used to compare

the entered password with the hashed password stored in the database.

2. **Creating the Users Table**: The `users` table must store user credentials securely. As part of our authentication system, we'll store passwords using hashing (covered below). Here's a simple structure for the `users` table:

sql

```sql
CREATE TABLE users (
    user_id  INT  AUTO_INCREMENT  PRIMARY KEY,
    first_name VARCHAR(100) NOT NULL,
    last_name VARCHAR(100) NOT NULL,
    email VARCHAR(255) UNIQUE NOT NULL,
    password VARCHAR(255) NOT NULL,  -- Store hashed passwords
    role ENUM('customer', 'admin') DEFAULT 'customer',
    created_at  TIMESTAMP  DEFAULT CURRENT_TIMESTAMP
);
```

- o `password`: This column stores the hashed password (not the plain text password).
- o `role`: This column defines the user's role (either `customer` or `admin`).

Creating User Roles (Admin, Customer)

In an e-commerce store, different users will have different roles. For example, **admins** will have the ability to manage products and orders, while **customers** will only be able to browse products and make purchases. We've already defined the role column in the users table, but now let's look at how we can create and manage these roles.

1. **Assigning Roles During Registration**: When a new user registers, you can assign them a default role of "customer." If needed, you can allow admins to manually assign roles during user registration or via the admin panel.

2. **Restricting Access Based on Roles**: In the login.php script, we check the user's role after successful login:

php

```php
if ($user['role'] == 'admin') {
    header("Location: admin/index.php");
} else {
    header("Location: home.php");
}
```

o **Admin Access**: If the user's role is admin, they are redirected to the admin dashboard (admin/index.php).

65

- o **Customer Access**: If the user's role is `customer`, they are redirected to the main shopping page (`home.php`).

3. **Displaying Content Based on Roles**: You can also restrict access to certain pages based on the user's role. For example, only admins should be able to view the admin panel.

php

```php
if ($_SESSION['user_role'] == 'admin') {
    // Show admin content
} else {
    // Show customer content
}
```

Implementing Password Hashing and Secure Authentication

Security is crucial in any user authentication system, especially for e-commerce sites where sensitive information is involved. Storing passwords securely is one of the most important aspects of building a secure authentication system.

1. **Password Hashing**: Instead of storing user passwords as plain text in the database, we store a hashed version of the password. PHP provides the `password_hash` function to securely hash passwords and the `password_verify` function to check passwords during login.

   - o **Hashing Passwords During Registration**:

```
php

if (isset($_POST['register'])) {
    $email = $_POST['email'];
    $password = $_POST['password'];
    $hashed_password              =
password_hash($password,
PASSWORD_DEFAULT);    // Hash the
password

    include '../config/db.php'; //
Include the database connection

    // Query to insert user details
    $sql = "INSERT INTO users (email,
password) VALUES (?, ?)";
    $stmt = $conn->prepare($sql);
    $stmt->bind_param("ss", $email,
$hashed_password);
    $stmt->execute();
}
```

- password_hash($password,
  PASSWORD_DEFAULT): This function
  hashes the password using a secure
  algorithm (bcrypt by default).
- The hashed password is stored in the
  password column of the users table.

2. **Verifying Passwords During Login**: When a user logs in, their entered password must be compared to the hashed password stored in the database. Use `password_verify` for this purpose.

```php
if               (password_verify($password,
$user['password'])) {
    // Password is correct, start the
session and redirect the user
}
```

- o `password_verify($password,` `$hashed_password)`: This function compares the entered password with the hashed password and returns `true` if they match.

3. **Session Management**: After a successful login, you can store the user's information in session variables to track the user's authentication state.

```php
session_start(); // Start the session
$_SESSION['user_id'] = $user['user_id'];
$_SESSION['user_email'] = $user['email'];
$_SESSION['user_role'] = $user['role'];
```

o **Session Variables**: These variables store the user's ID, email, and role, allowing the system to recognize the logged-in user on subsequent requests.

4. **Logging Out**: When the user logs out, you can destroy the session to log them out securely.

php

```php
session_start();
session_unset();    // Remove all session variables
session_destroy(); // Destroy the session
header("Location: login.php");
exit();
```

Conclusion

By the end of this chapter, you should have a secure user authentication system in place for your e-commerce store. You learned how to create a login system using PHP and MySQL, handle different user roles (admin and customer), and implement password hashing for secure authentication. This system ensures that only authorized users can access certain parts of the site and that their credentials are protected. With this foundation, you can further enhance the user management system, adding features like user registration, password resets, and email verification as needed.

CHAPTER 7

BUILDING THE PRODUCT CATALOG

In this chapter, we will focus on building a **Product Catalog** for your e-commerce store. The catalog will allow you to manage products, including adding, editing, and deleting items. We will also discuss how to organize products with categories and tags, as well as implement a search and filtering system to help customers find what they are looking for.

Adding, Editing, and Deleting Products

A key feature of any e-commerce store is the ability to manage products. As an admin, you should be able to add new products, edit existing products, and delete products when necessary. Let's go through how to build this functionality.

1. **Adding Products**: To add a product, we will create an **Add Product** form that takes input for the product name, description, price, stock quantity, image, and category. This information will be stored in the `products` table.

    File: `/admin/add-product.php`:

php

```php
<?php
session_start();
if ($_SESSION['user_role'] !== 'admin') {
    // Redirect non-admin users
    header("Location: login.php");
    exit();
}

include '../config/db.php';

if (isset($_POST['add_product'])) {
    $name = $_POST['name'];
    $description = $_POST['description'];
    $price = $_POST['price'];
    $stock_quantity           =
$_POST['stock_quantity'];
    $category_id = $_POST['category_id'];
    $image = $_FILES['image']['name'];
    $image_temp               =
$_FILES['image']['tmp_name'];

    // Upload the image to the uploads
directory
    move_uploaded_file($image_temp,
"../uploads/" . $image);
```

```php
$sql = "INSERT INTO products (name,
description, price, stock_quantity, image,
category_id)
        VALUES (?, ?, ?, ?, ?, ?)";

$stmt = $conn->prepare($sql);
$stmt->bind_param("ssdiss",    $name,
$description,   $price,   $stock_quantity,
$image, $category_id);
    if ($stmt->execute()) {
        echo        "Product        added
successfully!";
    } else {
        echo "Error: " . $stmt->error;
    }
}

?>

<form                       method="POST"
enctype="multipart/form-data">
    <label             for="name">Product
Name:</label>
    <input    type="text"    name="name"
required>
    <label
for="description">Description:</label>
    <textarea        name="description"
required></textarea>
```

```
<label for="price">Price:</label>
<input type="text" name="price" required>
<label for="stock_quantity">Stock Quantity:</label>
<input type="number" name="stock_quantity" required>
<label for="category_id">Category:</label>
<select name="category_id" required>
    <?php
    $sql = "SELECT * FROM categories";
    $result = $conn->query($sql);
    while ($category = $result->fetch_assoc()) {
        echo "<option value='" . $category['category_id'] . "'>" . $category['name'] . "</option>";
    }
    ?>
</select>
<label for="image">Product Image:</label>
<input type="file" name="image" required>
<button type="submit" name="add_product">Add Product</button>
</form>
```

o **Form Fields**: This form collects the product's name, description, price, stock quantity, category, and image. The image is uploaded to the server using $_FILES.

o **Database Insertion**: The product data is inserted into the products table using a prepared statement.

o **Image Upload**: The uploaded image is moved from the temporary folder to the uploads directory.

2. **Editing Products**: The ability to edit product details is crucial for managing your store. We'll create an **Edit Product** form that pre-fills existing product details.

File: /admin/edit-product.php:

php

```php
<?php
session_start();
if ($_SESSION['user_role'] !== 'admin') {
    header("Location: login.php");
    exit();
}

include '../config/db.php';

if (isset($_GET['id'])) {
```

```php
$product_id = $_GET['id'];

$sql = "SELECT * FROM products WHERE
product_id = ?";
$stmt = $conn->prepare($sql);
$stmt->bind_param("i", $product_id);
$stmt->execute();
$result = $stmt->get_result();
$product = $result->fetch_assoc();
}


if (isset($_POST['update_product'])) {
$name = $_POST['name'];
$description = $_POST['description'];
$price = $_POST['price'];
$stock_quantity                        =
$_POST['stock_quantity'];
$category_id = $_POST['category_id'];
$image = $_FILES['image']['name'];
$image_temp                            =
$_FILES['image']['tmp_name'];

if ($image) {
move_uploaded_file($image_temp,
"../uploads/" . $image);
$sql = "UPDATE products SET name =
?, description = ?, price = ?,
stock_quantity = ?, image = ?, category_id
= ? WHERE product_id = ?";
```

```php
        $stmt = $conn->prepare($sql);
        $stmt->bind_param("ssdissi",
$name,        $description,        $price,
$stock_quantity,  $image,  $category_id,
$product_id);
    } else {
        $sql = "UPDATE products SET name =
?,   description  =  ?,   price  =  ?,
stock_quantity = ?, category_id = ? WHERE
product_id = ?";
        $stmt = $conn->prepare($sql);
        $stmt->bind_param("ssdiss", $name,
$description,   $price,   $stock_quantity,
$category_id, $product_id);
    }

    if ($stmt->execute()) {
        echo        "Product        updated
successfully!";
    } else {
        echo "Error: " . $stmt->error;
    }
}
?>


<form                        method="POST"
enctype="multipart/form-data">
    <label            for="name">Product
Name:</label>
```

```php
    <input      type="text"      name="name"
value="<?php  echo  $product['name'];  ?>"
required>
    <label
for="description">Description:</label>
    <textarea            name="description"
required><?php                         echo
$product['description']; ?></textarea>
    <label for="price">Price:</label>
    <input      type="text"      name="price"
value="<?php  echo  $product['price'];  ?>"
required>
    <label      for="stock_quantity">Stock
Quantity:</label>
    <input                type="number"
name="stock_quantity"  value="<?php   echo
$product['stock_quantity']; ?>" required>
    <label
for="category_id">Category:</label>
    <select name="category_id" required>
        <?php
        $sql = "SELECT * FROM categories";
        $result = $conn->query($sql);
        while  ($category  =  $result-
>fetch_assoc()) {
            echo   "<option   value='"   .
$category['category_id']   .   "'"   "   .
($category['category_id']              ==
```

```
$product['category_id'] ? 'selected' : '')
. ">" . $category['name'] . "</option>";
        }
        ?>
    </select>
    <label              for="image">Product
Image:</label>
    <input type="file" name="image">
    <button                  type="submit"
name="update_product">Update
Product</button>
</form>
```

- o **Pre-filling the Form**: The form is pre-filled with the current product's details fetched from the database.
- o **Updating the Product**: If a new image is uploaded, it replaces the old one; otherwise, the product data is updated without changing the image.

3. **Deleting Products**: To allow admins to delete products, we will create a **Delete Product** functionality.

File: /admin/delete-product.php:

php

```php
<?php
session_start();
```

```php
if ($_SESSION['user_role'] !== 'admin') {
    header("Location: login.php");
    exit();
}

include '../config/db.php';

if (isset($_GET['id'])) {
    $product_id = $_GET['id'];

    $sql = "DELETE FROM products WHERE
product_id = ?";
    $stmt = $conn->prepare($sql);
    $stmt->bind_param("i", $product_id);
    if ($stmt->execute()) {
        echo        "Product        deleted
successfully!";
    } else {
        echo "Error: " . $stmt->error;
    }
}
?>
```

- o **Deleting a Product**: The product is deleted from the products table using the DELETE SQL query.

Categories and Tags for Organizing Products

To make it easier for customers to browse and filter products, we will organize products into **categories** and allow them to have **tags**.

1. **Categories Table**: The `categories` table stores product categories like "Electronics," "Clothing," etc.

   sql

   ```sql
   CREATE TABLE categories (
       category_id INT AUTO_INCREMENT PRIMARY KEY,
       name VARCHAR(255) NOT NULL
   );
   ```

2. **Tags Table**: The `tags` table stores product tags, which can help in categorizing products based on attributes like "Sale," "New Arrival," etc.

   sql

   ```sql
   CREATE TABLE tags (
       tag_id INT AUTO_INCREMENT PRIMARY KEY,
       name VARCHAR(255) NOT NULL
   );
   ```

3. **Linking Products to Categories and Tags**:

80

o **Categories**: As shown in the previous code snippets, products are linked to categories via the `category_id` foreign key in the `products` table.

o **Tags**: You can create a many-to-many relationship between products and tags by using a junction table.

```sql
CREATE TABLE product_tags (
    product_id INT NOT NULL,
    tag_id INT NOT NULL,
    FOREIGN KEY (product_id) REFERENCES products(product_id),
    FOREIGN KEY (tag_id) REFERENCES tags(tag_id)
);
```

Searching and Filtering Products

Finally, we need to implement a search and filtering system for customers to find products quickly. We can allow users to search by product name, category, or tags.

1. **Search Form**: Create a search form where users can enter a keyword to search for products.

   File: `/products/search.php`:

php

```
<form method="GET" action="search.php">
    <input    type="text"    name="search"
placeholder="Search for products...">
    <button type="submit">Search</button>
</form>
```

2. **Search Results**: When the form is submitted, use PHP to query the database and display products that match the search term.

php

```php
<?php
if (isset($_GET['search'])) {
    $search = $_GET['search'];
    $sql = "SELECT * FROM products WHERE
name LIKE ? OR description LIKE ?";
    $stmt = $conn->prepare($sql);
    $search_term = "%" . $search . "%";
    $stmt->bind_param("ss", $search_term,
$search_term);
    $stmt->execute();
    $result = $stmt->get_result();

    if ($result->num_rows > 0) {
        while ($product = $result-
>fetch_assoc()) {
```

```php
            echo "<div class='product'>";
            echo "<h3>" . $product['name']
. "</h3>";
            echo            "<p>"            .
$product['description'] . "</p>";
            echo      "<p>Price:      $"      .
$product['price'] . "</p>";
            echo "</div>";
        }
    } else {
        echo "No products found.";
    }
}
?>
```

3. **Filtering by Category or Tag**: You can allow users to filter products by category or tag by creating dropdown menus for categories and tags.

```php
php

<form method="GET" action="filter.php">
    <select name="category_id">
        <!-- Populate categories from the
database -->
    </select>
    <select name="tag_id">
        <!-- Populate tags from the
database -->
```

```
</select>
<button type="submit">Filter</button>
</form>
```

Then, in the filtering script (`filter.php`), you can query the products based on the selected category or tag.

By the end of this chapter, you will have a fully functional **Product Catalog** that allows you to add, edit, delete, and manage products. The catalog will be organized using categories and tags, and customers will be able to search and filter products to find what they need quickly.

CHAPTER 8

SHOPPING CART FUNCTIONALITY

The shopping cart is one of the most critical features of any e-commerce store. It allows customers to add products, modify quantities, and proceed to checkout. In this chapter, we will build a simple shopping cart system using PHP. We'll store the cart data in **sessions**, allowing the cart to persist as the customer browses different pages. Additionally, we'll cover how to update product quantities and remove items from the cart.

Implementing a Simple Shopping Cart System

1. **Setting Up the Cart**: A shopping cart will store the product IDs, names, quantities, and prices of the items a customer adds. We'll use PHP sessions to store the cart data, allowing the cart to be persistent across different pages.

   Start the session: In order to use sessions, we must call `session_start()` at the beginning of the PHP script. This allows us to access and modify session variables.

   php

85

```
session_start();  // Start the session to
store cart data
```

2. **Adding Products to the Cart**: When a user clicks on the "Add to Cart" button, the product is added to their cart. The product's ID, name, price, and quantity are stored in the session.

File: /cart/add-to-cart.php:

php

```php
<?php
session_start();

// Assuming that the product ID and
quantity are passed via GET or POST
if     (isset($_GET['product_id'])      &&
isset($_GET['quantity'])) {
    $product_id = $_GET['product_id'];
    $quantity = $_GET['quantity'];

    // Fetch the product details from the
database
    include '../config/db.php';
    $sql = "SELECT * FROM products WHERE
product_id = ?";
    $stmt = $conn->prepare($sql);
```

```php
$stmt->bind_param("i", $product_id);
$stmt->execute();
$result = $stmt->get_result();

if ($result->num_rows > 0) {
    $product = $result->fetch_assoc();

    // Create a cart item with product
details
    $cart_item = [
        'product_id'                    =>
$product['product_id'],
        'name' => $product['name'],
        'price' => $product['price'],
        'quantity' => $quantity,
    ];

    // If the cart doesn't exist,
create it
    if (!isset($_SESSION['cart'])) {
        $_SESSION['cart'] = [];
    }

    // Check if the product is already
in the cart
    $found = false;
    foreach ($_SESSION['cart'] as
&$item) {
```

```php
            if    ($item['product_id']    ==
$product_id) {
                $item['quantity']         +=
$quantity;   // Update the quantity if the
product is already in the cart
                $found = true;
                break;
            }
        }


        // If the product is not found in
the cart, add it
        if (!$found) {
            $_SESSION['cart'][]            =
$cart_item;
        }

        echo "Product added to cart!";
    }
}
?>
```

- o **Adding to Cart**: The product is added to the cart session array. If the product already exists in the cart, its quantity is updated.
- o **Session Storage**: The cart data is stored in the session variable `$_SESSION['cart']`. This allows the cart to persist as the user navigates through the site.

3. **Viewing the Cart**: To display the contents of the shopping cart, we need to create a page that retrieves the cart data from the session and presents it to the user.

File: /cart/view-cart.php:

php

```php
<?php
session_start();

if      (isset($_SESSION['cart'])      &&
!empty($_SESSION['cart'])) {
    echo "<h2>Your Shopping Cart</h2>";
    echo "<table border='1'>";
    echo
"<tr><th>Product</th><th>Price</th><th>Qu
antity</th><th>Total</th><th>Action</th><
/tr>";

    $total = 0;
    foreach ($_SESSION['cart'] as $item) {
        $item_total   =   $item['price']   *
$item['quantity'];
        $total += $item_total;

        echo "<tr>";
        echo   "<td>"   .   $item['name']   .
"</td>";
```

```php
        echo            "<td>$"     .
number_format($item['price'],      2)     .
"</td>";
        echo "<td>" . $item['quantity'] .
"</td>";
        echo            "<td>$"     .
number_format($item_total, 2) . "</td>";
        echo   "<td><a   href='remove-from-
cart.php?product_id="                     .
$item['product_id'] . "'>Remove</a></td>";
        echo "</tr>";
    }

    echo                        "<tr><td
colspan='3'>Total</td><td>$"              .
number_format($total,           2)        .
"</td><td></td></tr>";
    echo "</table>";
    echo   "<a   href='checkout.php'>Proceed
to Checkout</a>";
} else {
    echo "Your cart is empty.";
}
?>
```

- o **Displaying Cart Items**: The cart contents are retrieved from the session and displayed in a table with columns for the product name, price, quantity, and total price.

90

o   **Removing Items**: A link is provided to remove items from the cart. When the user clicks the "Remove" link, the product is deleted from the session.

Storing Cart Data Using Sessions

We are using PHP sessions to store the shopping cart data. Sessions allow us to store data that persists across multiple pages during a user's visit to the site.

- **Session Variables**: `$_SESSION['cart']` holds the array of products in the cart. This allows the cart data to persist while the user navigates between pages, like viewing the product catalog, checking out, etc.
- **Session Initialization**: Always call `session_start()` at the beginning of each PHP script where you need to access session data. Without this, you won't be able to access or modify session variables.

Updating Product Quantities and Removing Items from the Cart

1. **Updating Product Quantities**: The quantity of a product in the cart can be updated if the user changes the quantity in the cart. We will add functionality to modify the quantity of a product.

File: `/cart/update-cart.php`:

php

```php
<?php
session_start();

if (isset($_POST['update_cart'])) {
    $product_id = $_POST['product_id'];
    $new_quantity = $_POST['quantity'];

    // Find the product in the cart and update its quantity
    foreach ($_SESSION['cart'] as &$item) {
        if ($item['product_id'] == $product_id) {
            $item['quantity'] = $new_quantity;
            break;
        }
    }

    echo "Cart updated!";
}
?>
```

- o **Updating Quantity**: This script checks for the product_id and quantity passed via a form and updates the corresponding item in the cart. If the product is not in the cart, it won't update anything.

Form for Updating Quantities:

php

```
<form     method="POST"     action="update-
cart.php">
    <input   type="number"   name="quantity"
value="<?php  echo  $item['quantity'];  ?>"
min="1">
    <input type="hidden" name="product_id"
value="<?php   echo   $item['product_id'];
?>">
    <button                  type="submit"
name="update_cart">Update
Quantity</button>
</form>
```

2. **Removing Items from the Cart**: The cart also needs the ability to remove products. When a user clicks the "Remove" link, the product is deleted from the session.

File: `/cart/remove-from-cart.php`:

php

```
<?php
session_start();
```

```php
if (isset($_GET['product_id'])) {
    $product_id = $_GET['product_id'];

    // Remove the product from the cart
    foreach ($_SESSION['cart'] as $key =>
$item) {
        if    ($item['product_id']    ==
$product_id) {

unset($_SESSION['cart'][$key]);  // Remove
the item from the cart
            break;
        }
    }

    echo "Product removed from cart.";
}
?>
```

o **Removing Items**: The product is removed by
   finding its `product_id` in the session and using
   `unset()` to delete it from the cart array.

Conclusion

By the end of this chapter, you will have implemented a **simple
shopping cart system** for your e-commerce store. The cart allows
users to add products, view the cart, update quantities, and remove

items. Using PHP sessions to store the cart data ensures that the cart persists across different pages while the user browses the site. This forms the foundation for further development, such as adding checkout functionality, applying discounts, or integrating with payment gateways.

CHAPTER 9

CHECKOUT AND ORDER MANAGEMENT

The checkout process is one of the most important steps in an e-commerce website. It involves collecting customer information, processing their order, and confirming the purchase. In this chapter, we will build the checkout page, including the order summary, address collection, and shipping options. We will also implement order management features such as tracking order status and maintaining an order history.

Creating a Checkout Page with Order Summary

The checkout page allows the customer to review their cart, enter their shipping information, and proceed with the payment process. We'll display an order summary with product details and a total price.

1. **Order Summary Page**: On the checkout page, we will display the products in the cart, their quantities, the price of each item, and the total price of the order.

   File: /cart/checkout.php:

php

```php
<?php
session_start();

if      (!isset($_SESSION['cart'])      ||
empty($_SESSION['cart'])) {
    echo "Your cart is empty.";
    exit();
}

// Calculate the total price
$total = 0;
foreach ($_SESSION['cart'] as $item) {
    $total    +=     $item['price']    *
$item['quantity'];
}
?>

<h2>Order Summary</h2>
<table border="1">

<tr><th>Product</th><th>Price</th><th>Qua
ntity</th><th>Total</th></tr>
    <?php
    foreach ($_SESSION['cart'] as $item) {
        $item_total   =   $item['price']   *
$item['quantity'];
        echo "<tr>";
```

```php
        echo "<td>" . $item['name'] .
"</td>";
        echo "<td>$" .
number_format($item['price'], 2) .
"</td>";
        echo "<td>" . $item['quantity'] .
"</td>";
        echo "<td>$" .
number_format($item_total, 2) . "</td>";
        echo "</tr>";
    }
    ?>
    <tr><td
colspan="3">Total</td><td>$<?php echo
number_format($total, 2); ?></td></tr>
</table>

<form method="POST" action="process-
order.php">
    <label for="address">Shipping
Address:</label>
    <textarea name="address"
required></textarea><br>

    <label for="shipping">Shipping
Option:</label>
    <select name="shipping" required>
        <option value="standard">Standard
Shipping (5-7 days) - $5.00</option>
```

```
    <option    value="express">Express
Shipping (2-3 days) - $15.00</option>
    </select><br>

    <button              type="submit"
name="place_order">Place Order</button>
    </form>
```

- o **Order Summary**: This page fetches the cart details from the session and displays a summary of the products, their prices, quantities, and the total price.
- o **Shipping Address and Options**: Customers are asked to enter a shipping address and choose a shipping option. Shipping options include "Standard" and "Express" shipping, with different prices for each option.

2. **Placing an Order**: When the customer submits the order, the form data is sent to the `process-order.php` script, where the order is processed, and the order details are stored in the database.

Implementing Address Collection and Shipping Options

The next step is to collect the customer's shipping information, including their address and preferred shipping method. These details will be stored in the `orders` table, along with the order's status and total price.

1. **Order Processing**: When the customer places an order, we need to insert the order information (such as products, total price, shipping details, and user ID) into the `orders` table.

File: /cart/process-order.php:

php

```php
<?php
session_start();

if (!isset($_SESSION['user_id'])) {
    echo "You must be logged in to place an
order.";
    exit();
}

if (isset($_POST['place_order'])) {
    $user_id = $_SESSION['user_id'];
    $address = $_POST['address'];
    $shipping = $_POST['shipping'];
    $total_price = 0;

    // Calculate the total price from the
cart
    foreach ($_SESSION['cart'] as $item) {
        $total_price += $item['price'] *
$item['quantity'];
```

```php
    }


    // Insert the order into the orders
table
    include '../config/db.php';
    $sql = "INSERT INTO orders (user_id,
total_price,       shipping,       address,
order_status)    VALUES    (?,   ?,   ?,   ?,
'pending')";
    $stmt = $conn->prepare($sql);
    $stmt->bind_param("dsss",    $user_id,
$total_price, $shipping, $address);


    if ($stmt->execute()) {
        $order_id = $stmt->insert_id;


        // Insert each product into the
order_details table
        foreach    ($_SESSION['cart']    as
$item) {
            $sql    =    "INSERT    INTO
order_details    (order_id,    product_id,
quantity, price) VALUES (?, ?, ?, ?)";
            $stmt = $conn->prepare($sql);
            $stmt->bind_param("iiid",
$order_id,           $item['product_id'],
$item['quantity'], $item['price']);
            $stmt->execute();
        }
```

```
        // Clear the cart after placing the
order
        unset($_SESSION['cart']);

        echo "Order placed successfully!
Your order ID is: " . $order_id;
    } else {
        echo "Error: " . $stmt->error;
    }
}
?>
```

- o **Inserting Order**: The order details (user ID, total price, shipping option, and address) are inserted into the `orders` table.
- o **Inserting Order Details**: Each product in the cart is inserted into the `order_details` table, which links products to specific orders.
- o **Clearing the Cart**: After placing the order, the cart is cleared by unsetting the `$_SESSION['cart']` variable.

2. **Shipping Information**: The `shipping` field in the `orders` table stores the chosen shipping option (e.g., "Standard" or "Express"). This can be used to calculate delivery times or additional charges.

Managing Order Status and Order History

Once the order is placed, it's important to track its progress through different stages, such as "pending," "shipped," and "delivered." Admin users should be able to view and update the status of each order. Customers should be able to view their order history.

1. **Order Status**: The `orders` table has an `order_status` column, which tracks the current status of an order. Common statuses include:

    o **Pending**: The order has been placed but not yet processed.

    o **Shipped**: The order has been dispatched.

    o **Delivered**: The order has been delivered to the customer.

    o **Cancelled**: The order was cancelled.

File: /admin/manage-orders.php:

php

```php
<?php
session_start();
if ($_SESSION['user_role'] !== 'admin') {
    header("Location: login.php");
    exit();
}
```

```php
include '../config/db.php';

// Fetch all orders from the database
$sql = "SELECT * FROM orders";
$result = $conn->query($sql);

echo "<h2>Manage Orders</h2>";
echo "<table border='1'>";
echo "<tr><th>Order ID</th><th>User</th><th>Total</th><th>Status</th><th>Action</th></tr>";

while ($order = $result->fetch_assoc()) {
    echo "<tr>";
    echo "<td>" . $order['order_id'] . "</td>";
    echo "<td>" . $order['user_id'] . "</td>";
    echo "<td>$" . number_format($order['total_price'], 2) . "</td>";
    echo "<td>" . $order['order_status'] . "</td>";
    echo "<td><a href='update-order-status.php?order_id=" . $order['order_id'] . "'>Update Status</a></td>";
    echo "</tr>";
}
```

```
echo "</table>";
?>
```

- o **Managing Orders**: The admin can view all orders and their current status. Admins can update the status of each order.

2. **Updating Order Status**: To allow admins to update the status of an order, we will create a page that enables them to change the order status from "pending" to "shipped" or "delivered."

File: /admin/update-order-status.php:

php

```php
<?php
session_start();
if ($_SESSION['user_role'] !== 'admin') {
    header("Location: login.php");
    exit();
}

include '../config/db.php';

if (isset($_GET['order_id'])) {
    $order_id = $_GET['order_id'];

    // Fetch the order details
```

```php
    $sql = "SELECT * FROM orders WHERE
order_id = ?";
    $stmt = $conn->prepare($sql);
    $stmt->bind_param("i", $order_id);
    $stmt->execute();
    $result = $stmt->get_result();
    $order = $result->fetch_assoc();
}


if (isset($_POST['update_status'])) {
    $new_status = $_POST['order_status'];

    $sql = "UPDATE orders SET order_status
= ? WHERE order_id = ?";
    $stmt = $conn->prepare($sql);
    $stmt->bind_param("si",   $new_status,
$order_id);
    $stmt->execute();

    echo "Order status updated!";
}
?>

<form method="POST">
    <label        for="order_status">Order
Status:</label>
    <select name="order_status">
```

```
        <option value="pending" <?php echo
($order['order_status'] == 'pending' ?
'selected' : ''); ?>>Pending</option>
        <option value="shipped" <?php echo
($order['order_status'] == 'shipped' ?
'selected' : ''); ?>>Shipped</option>
        <option value="delivered" <?php
echo ($order['order_status'] ==
'delivered' ? 'selected' : '');
?>>Delivered</option>
        <option value="cancelled" <?php
echo ($order['order_status'] ==
'cancelled' ? 'selected' : '');
?>>Cancelled</option>
    </select>
    <button               type="submit"
name="update_status">Update
Status</button>
</form>
```

- o **Updating Order Status**: The admin can update the order status to "pending," "shipped," "delivered," or "cancelled."

3. **Viewing Order History**: Customers should be able to view their own order history on their account page. The following query retrieves a customer's orders:

File: /users/order-history.php:

107

php

```php
<?php
session_start();

if (!isset($_SESSION['user_id'])) {
    echo "Please log in to view your order
history.";
    exit();
}

$user_id = $_SESSION['user_id'];
include '../config/db.php';

// Fetch the user's orders
$sql = "SELECT * FROM orders WHERE user_id
= ?";
$stmt = $conn->prepare($sql);
$stmt->bind_param("i", $user_id);
$stmt->execute();
$result = $stmt->get_result();

echo "<h2>Your Order History</h2>";
while ($order = $result->fetch_assoc()) {
    echo "<p>Order ID: " .
$order['order_id'] . " - Status: " .
$order['order_status'] . " - Total: $" .
number_format($order['total_price'], 2) .
"</p>";
```

```
}
?>
```

  o **Order History**: The customer can view their past
     orders and the current status of each order.

By the end of this chapter, you will have implemented a full
checkout and order management system. Customers can place
orders, select shipping options, and enter their address. Admins
can manage orders, update statuses, and track the history of each
order. This functionality is crucial for ensuring a smooth shopping
experience and efficient order fulfillment.

CHAPTER 10

PAYMENT INTEGRATION WITH PHP

One of the most essential steps in building an e-commerce store is integrating a secure payment gateway. Payment gateways allow your customers to pay for their orders through online methods like credit/debit cards, PayPal, and other services. In this chapter, we'll explore the integration of popular payment gateways (e.g., PayPal, Stripe) with PHP, securely handle transactions, and use APIs to process payments.

Overview of Payment Gateways (PayPal, Stripe, etc.)

A **payment gateway** is a service that authorizes and processes payments for e-commerce transactions. It acts as a middleman between your online store and the payment processor (banks or financial institutions), ensuring secure transactions.

Some popular payment gateways include:

1. **PayPal**:
   - PayPal is one of the most widely used online payment systems. It allows users to pay with their PayPal account, credit cards, or bank transfers.

110

o PayPal offers multiple integration methods, including direct API integration, PayPal Buttons, and its own SDKs.

2. **Stripe**:

o Stripe is a popular payment processor known for its simple API and flexibility. It allows you to accept payments via credit cards, debit cards, and digital wallets.

o Stripe's API supports a wide variety of payment methods and currencies, making it a great choice for global businesses.

3. **Authorize.Net**:

o Another widely used gateway, especially in the United States, Authorize.Net offers a flexible API for accepting payments via credit cards, e-checks, and digital wallets.

4. **Square**:

o Square is often used by small businesses and offers both online and in-person payment processing. It has a simple API for integrating payments into your site.

Each payment gateway has its pros and cons, but the most popular choices are **PayPal** and **Stripe** because of their ease of use, reliability, and broad customer base.

Securely Handling Transactions with PHP

Security is a top priority when processing payments. The payment gateway will typically handle most of the sensitive data (like credit card details), but as a developer, there are several steps you should follow to ensure secure transactions:

1. **Use HTTPS (SSL/TLS)**: Ensure your website uses **SSL/TLS encryption** to secure the connection between the customer and the server. This ensures that sensitive data (e.g., credit card details) is encrypted and cannot be intercepted by attackers.

   o SSL (Secure Sockets Layer) or TLS (Transport Layer Security) certificates are required to establish a secure connection.

   o Your e-commerce store must be accessible through **HTTPS** (e.g., `https://yourdomain.com`) rather than HTTP.

2. **Never Store Sensitive Data**: For compliance with security standards (e.g., **PCI DSS**), never store sensitive payment details such as full credit card numbers or CVV codes on your server. Instead, use tokenization, a method in which the sensitive data is replaced with a token that can be used for future transactions.

3. **Use Secure Payment API Integrations**: Both PayPal and Stripe offer secure API integrations that ensure

customer payment details are processed through their platforms. Use their official SDKs or libraries to handle sensitive data, ensuring the payment information never touches your server.

4. **Two-Factor Authentication (2FA)**: Enable **2FA** for any administrative panel related to payment processing. This ensures that even if login credentials are compromised, unauthorized users cannot access the payment information.

5. **Error Handling and Logging**: Always implement proper error handling and logging when integrating payment gateways. Avoid exposing sensitive error messages to customers, and ensure that all payment transactions are logged securely for auditing and troubleshooting purposes.

Using APIs to Process Payments

Payment gateways like **PayPal** and **Stripe** provide APIs to allow e-commerce stores to process payments securely. Let's dive into how we can integrate each of these gateways into your PHP-based e-commerce store.

PayPal Payment Integration

To integrate PayPal, you'll use their **PayPal REST API**. PayPal offers an SDK and easy-to-follow documentation for integrating payment buttons and handling transactions.

1. **Creating a PayPal Developer Account**:
   - Go to the PayPal Developer Portal and create a developer account.
   - Create a new **REST API app** to get your **Client ID** and **Secret** for authentication.

2. **Installing the PayPal SDK**: PayPal provides a PHP SDK that simplifies integration. You can install the PayPal SDK using Composer, which is the recommended way to manage dependencies in PHP.

   Run this command to install the SDK via Composer:

```bash
composer require paypal/rest-api-sdk-php
```

3. **Setting Up the PayPal Payment Flow**: Once you have the PayPal SDK installed, you can create a payment page for customers to make payments.

   File: /cart/paypal-checkout.php:

```php
<?php
```

114

```php
session_start();

// PayPal API credentials
define('PAYPAL_CLIENT_ID',
'your_client_id');
define('PAYPAL_SECRET', 'your_secret');
define('PAYPAL_SANDBOX', true);    // Use
true for sandbox, false for live

require 'vendor/autoload.php';

// Create PayPal API context
$apiContext = new \PayPal\Rest\ApiContext(
    new \PayPal\Auth\OAuthTokenCredential(
        PAYPAL_CLIENT_ID,
        PAYPAL_SECRET
    )
);

// Create a payment request
$payer = new \PayPal\Api\Payer();
$payer->setPaymentMethod('paypal');

$amount = new \PayPal\Api\Amount();
$amount->setCurrency('USD')
       ->setTotal($_SESSION['total']);  //
Total amount to be paid
```

```php
$transaction                =                new
\PayPal\Api\Transaction();
$transaction->setAmount($amount)
        ->setDescription('Order
payment');

$redirectUrls               =                new
\PayPal\Api\RedirectUrls();
$redirectUrls-
>setReturnUrl('http://yourwebsite.com/pay
ment-success.php')
                  -
>setCancelUrl('http://yourwebsite.com/pay
ment-cancel.php');

$payment = new \PayPal\Api\Payment();
$payment->setIntent('sale')
        ->setPayer($payer)
        ->setTransactions([$transaction])
        ->setRedirectUrls($redirectUrls);

try {
    $payment->create($apiContext);
    // Redirect the user to PayPal for
approval
    header("Location:   "  .  $payment-
>getApprovalLink());
} catch (Exception $e) {
    die($e);
```

```
}
?>
```

- o **Creating the Payment**: We set up a payer, transaction details, and redirect URLs.
- o **Redirecting to PayPal**: After creating the payment, we redirect the customer to PayPal to approve the transaction.

4. **Handling Payment Confirmation**: Once the customer approves the payment, PayPal will redirect them back to the specified `return_url`. In the `payment-success.php` file, you need to capture the payment details.

File: /cart/payment-success.php:

php

```php
<?php
session_start();
require 'vendor/autoload.php';

if      (isset($_GET['paymentId'])        &&
isset($_GET['PayerID'])) {
    $paymentId = $_GET['paymentId'];
    $payerId = $_GET['PayerID'];

    // Set up PayPal API context
```

```php
$apiContext              =              new
\PayPal\Rest\ApiContext(
     new
\PayPal\Auth\OAuthTokenCredential(
          PAYPAL_CLIENT_ID,
          PAYPAL_SECRET
     )
);

// Execute the payment
$payment                              =
\PayPal\Api\Payment::get($paymentId,
$apiContext);
$execution              =              new
\PayPal\Api\PaymentExecution();
$execution->setPayerId($payerId);

try {
     $payment->execute($execution,
$apiContext);
     echo "Payment successful!";
     // Update the order status in your
database
     // Empty the cart, etc.
} catch (Exception $e) {
     echo "Error: " . $e->getMessage();
}
} else {
   echo "Payment failed.";
```

```
    }
    ?>
```

- o **Payment Execution**: After the customer approves the payment, this script executes the payment and confirms that the payment was successful.
- o **Database Update**: You can update the order status and empty the shopping cart after the successful payment.

Stripe Payment Integration

Stripe is another popular payment gateway that is easy to integrate with PHP. It allows you to accept card payments directly on your website.

1. **Creating a Stripe Account**:
   - o Go to the Stripe website and create an account.
   - o After logging in, get your **API keys** from the API keys section.

2. **Installing the Stripe PHP SDK**: You can install the Stripe PHP SDK using Composer:

```bash
composer require stripe/stripe-php
```

3. **Processing Payments with Stripe**: To process payments using Stripe, you'll need to collect the customer's card information using Stripe's `Checkout` or `Elements` UI components.

File: /cart/stripe-checkout.php:

php

```php
<?php
session_start();

require 'vendor/autoload.php';

// Stripe API key
\Stripe\Stripe::setApiKey('your_stripe_se
cret_key');

// Create a payment intent
$intent = \Stripe\PaymentIntent::create([
    'amount' => $_SESSION['total'] * 100,
// Amount in cents
    'currency' => 'usd',
]);

?>

<form        action="payment-success.php"
method="POST">
```

```
    <script
src="https://checkout.stripe.com/checkout
.js"
            class="stripe-button"
            data-
key="your_stripe_publishable_key"
            data-amount="<?php       echo
$_SESSION['total'] * 100; ?>"
            data-name="Your Store Name"
            data-description="Order
Payment"
            data-locale="auto">
    </script>
</form>
```

- o **Creating a Payment Intent**: The payment intent is created with the total amount of the order. Stripe handles the rest of the payment process securely.

- o **Stripe Checkout**: Stripe's **Checkout** system automatically handles card input and validation for you.

4. **Handling Stripe Payment Confirmation**: After the payment is successfully processed, you can confirm the payment and store the order in your database.

File: /cart/payment-success.php:

php

```php
<?php
session_start();
require 'vendor/autoload.php';

\Stripe\Stripe::setApiKey('your_stripe_se
cret_key');

// Retrieve the PaymentIntent
$paymentIntent                          =
\Stripe\PaymentIntent::retrieve($_POST['p
ayment_intent']);

if ($paymentIntent->status == 'succeeded')
{
    echo "Payment successful!";
    // Update the order in the database
    // Empty the cart, etc.
} else {
    echo "Payment failed.";
}
?>
```

o **Confirming Payment**: This script retrieves the
   payment_intent ID from the POST data and
   checks its status. If the status is succeeded, the
   payment is complete, and you can proceed with
   order confirmation.

By the end of this chapter, you should have a fully functional **payment integration system** using PayPal or Stripe (or both). You will have securely processed payments, updated order status, and ensured the safety of your customers' financial information. The next step would be to expand on this with more complex features, such as recurring billing, refunds, and advanced fraud detection.

CHAPTER 11

MANAGING INVENTORY AND STOCK LEVELS

In this chapter, we will explore how to manage the inventory and stock levels for the products in your e-commerce store. Effective inventory management ensures that you always have the right amount of stock available to meet customer demand, without overstocking or running out of items. We'll cover implementing stock tracking for products, automatically updating stock levels after each order, and setting up alerts for low inventory and reordering.

Implementing Stock Tracking for Products

The first step in managing inventory is to track the available stock of each product in your database. Every time a customer places an order, the stock level for each ordered product needs to be adjusted accordingly.

1. **Add a Stock Column to the Products Table**: In your `products` table, you should already have a `stock_quantity` column. This column will track how many units of each product are available in your store.

Example schema for the `products` table (if not already done):

sql

```
CREATE TABLE products (
    product_id INT AUTO_INCREMENT PRIMARY KEY,
    name VARCHAR(255) NOT NULL,
    description TEXT,
    price DECIMAL(10, 2) NOT NULL,
    stock_quantity INT NOT NULL,
    image VARCHAR(255),
    category_id INT,
    created_at TIMESTAMP DEFAULT CURRENT_TIMESTAMP,
    FOREIGN KEY (category_id) REFERENCES categories(category_id)
);
```

- o `stock_quantity`: The number of units currently available for that product.

2. **Displaying Stock Information**: When displaying products on your site, it's a good practice to show customers how many items are left in stock or when they can expect the product to be available if it's out of stock. This helps create transparency and can influence purchase decisions.

File: /products/details.php:

```
php
```

```php
<?php
// Assuming that the product details are
retrieved from the database
echo    "<p>Stock    Available:    "    .
$product['stock_quantity'] . " units</p>";
?>
```

Automatically Updating Stock After Each Order

Once a customer places an order, we need to automatically decrease the stock quantity for each product they have ordered. This process should happen in real-time to ensure that stock levels are always up-to-date.

1. **Updating Stock When an Order is Placed**: After an order is successfully placed, we need to loop through the `order_details` table and update the `stock_quantity` of each ordered product. This ensures that the stock levels reflect the products sold.

   File: /cart/process-order.php (after order has been successfully placed):

   ```
   php
   ```

   ```php
   <?php
   ```

126

```php
session_start();

if (!isset($_SESSION['user_id'])) {
    echo "You must be logged in to place an
order.";
    exit();
}


if (isset($_POST['place_order'])) {
    $user_id = $_SESSION['user_id'];
    $address = $_POST['address'];
    $shipping = $_POST['shipping'];
    $total_price = 0;

    // Calculate the total price from the
cart
    foreach ($_SESSION['cart'] as $item) {
        $total_price += $item['price'] *
$item['quantity'];
    }

    include '../config/db.php';

    // Insert the order into the orders
table
    $sql = "INSERT INTO orders (user_id,
total_price,      shipping,      address,
order_status)    VALUES   (?,   ?,   ?,   ?,
'pending')";
```

```php
$stmt = $conn->prepare($sql);
$stmt->bind_param("dsss",    $user_id,
$total_price, $shipping, $address);

    if ($stmt->execute()) {
        $order_id = $stmt->insert_id;

        // Update the stock for each
product in the order
        foreach ($_SESSION['cart'] as
$item) {
            $product_id           =
$item['product_id'];
            $quantity = $item['quantity'];

        // Decrease the stock quantity
for each ordered product
            $update_stock_sql   = "UPDATE
products    SET    stock_quantity    =
stock_quantity - ? WHERE product_id = ?";
            $update_stmt       =    $conn-
>prepare($update_stock_sql);
            $update_stmt-
>bind_param("ii", $quantity, $product_id);
            $update_stmt->execute();

        // Insert each product into the
order_details table
```

```
            $sql    =    "INSERT    INTO
order_details    (order_id,    product_id,
quantity, price) VALUES (?, ?, ?, ?)";
            $stmt = $conn->prepare($sql);
            $stmt->bind_param("iiid",
$order_id,            $item['product_id'],
$item['quantity'], $item['price']);
            $stmt->execute();
        }


        // Clear the cart after placing the
order
        unset($_SESSION['cart']);


        echo  "Order  placed  successfully!
Your order ID is: " . $order_id;
    } else {
        echo "Error: " . $stmt->error;
    }
}
?>
```

- o **Decreasing Stock**: After each product is processed in the order, the stock_quantity is updated by subtracting the quantity of the product ordered.

2. **Preventing Over-Selling**: Before allowing a customer to add an item to their cart, check the available stock. If the

stock quantity is zero, inform the customer that the item is out of stock and prevent them from adding it to the cart.

File: /products/details.php (Before adding to cart):

php

```
if ($product['stock_quantity'] <= 0) {
    echo "<p>Sorry, this product is out of stock.</p>";
    echo "<button disabled>Add to Cart</button>";
} else {
    echo "<button>Add to Cart</button>";
}
```

- o **Stock Check**: Before allowing customers to add a product to the cart, check if the stock_quantity is greater than zero.

Alerts for Low Inventory and Reordering

To maintain smooth operations, it is important to monitor stock levels and alert the admin when stock is running low. This can help prevent running out of stock unexpectedly and allow for timely reordering.

1. **Setting a Low Stock Threshold**: Determine a minimum stock threshold for each product. When a product's stock falls below this threshold, an alert can be triggered.

   Example of a simple query to find low-stock products:

   sql

   ```sql
   SELECT * FROM products WHERE stock_quantity
   <= 5;
   ```

   - o   You can set the threshold to any value based on your business needs. In this example, we've set the threshold to 5.

2. **Alerting Admin for Low Stock**: Create a page in the admin panel that shows products with low stock. You can display a warning or send an email notification to the store admin.

   File: /admin/low-stock-alerts.php:

   php

   ```php
   <?php
   session_start();
   if ($_SESSION['user_role'] !== 'admin') {
       header("Location: login.php");
       exit();
   }
   ```

```php
include '../config/db.php';

// Query to find products with low stock
$sql = "SELECT * FROM products WHERE
stock_quantity <= 5";
$result = $conn->query($sql);

echo "<h2>Low Stock Products</h2>";
echo "<table border='1'>";
echo "<tr><th>Product Name</th><th>Stock
Quantity</th><th>Reorder</th></tr>";

while ($product = $result->fetch_assoc())
{
    echo "<tr>";
    echo "<td>" . $product['name'] .
"</td>";
    echo "<td>" .
$product['stock_quantity'] . "</td>";
    echo "<td><a href='reorder-
product.php?product_id=" .
$product['product_id'] .
"'>Reorder</a></td>";
    echo "</tr>";
}
echo "</table>";
?>
```

o **Displaying Low Stock**: The admin can view products that are running low on stock and take appropriate action.

3. **Automated Email Alerts**: For added convenience, you can implement email alerts that notify the admin when stock levels fall below a certain threshold. This can be done using PHP's `mail()` function or libraries like **PHPMailer**.

Example using PHPMailer:

```php
php

use PHPMailer\PHPMailer\PHPMailer;
use PHPMailer\PHPMailer\Exception;

require 'vendor/autoload.php';

$mail = new PHPMailer(true);

try {
    $mail->isSMTP();
    $mail->Host = 'smtp.example.com';
    $mail->SMTPAuth = true;
    $mail->Username =
'your_email@example.com';
    $mail->Password =
'your_email_password';
```

```
    $mail->SMTPSecure              =
PHPMailer::ENCRYPTION_STARTTLS;
    $mail->Port = 587;

    $mail->setFrom('no-
reply@yourstore.com', 'Your Store');
    $mail-
>addAddress('admin@example.com', 'Admin');

    $mail->Subject = 'Low Stock Alert';
    $mail->Body   = 'The following product
is low on stock: ' . $product['name'];

    $mail->send();
    echo  'Stock  alert  email  has  been
sent.';
} catch (Exception $e) {
    echo "Message could not be sent. Mailer
Error: {$mail->ErrorInfo}";
}
```

o **Email Notification**: When stock falls below the threshold, the admin is notified via email, so they can reorder the product promptly.

Conclusion

By the end of this chapter, you will have successfully implemented an inventory management system that tracks product stock levels in real-time. You'll be able to automatically update stock levels after each order, set alerts for low inventory, and allow admins to reorder products. These features ensure your e-commerce store can efficiently manage stock, reduce the risk of overselling, and maintain a smooth shopping experience for customers.

CHAPTER 12

BUILDING A RESPONSIVE DESIGN FOR MOBILE USERS

In this chapter, we will focus on creating a **responsive design** for your e-commerce store. A responsive design ensures that your website looks good and functions well across all devices, from desktop computers to smartphones and tablets. With the increasing number of mobile users, it's crucial to design your e-commerce site in a way that delivers an optimal browsing and shopping experience on any screen size.

Introduction to Responsive Web Design

Responsive web design (RWD) is a design approach that makes web pages render well on a variety of devices and window or screen sizes. Rather than creating separate websites for different devices (desktop, tablet, mobile), a responsive design adjusts the layout and elements based on the size of the screen viewing the page.

The key principles of responsive web design include:

1. **Fluid Grids**: Use flexible layouts that adapt to different screen sizes. This is achieved by using relative units like percentages rather than fixed units like pixels.

2. **Flexible Images**: Images should resize to fit different screen sizes without losing their quality or breaking the layout.

3. **Media Queries**: CSS techniques that allow you to apply styles based on the screen size or device type.

Responsive design is essential for e-commerce because users expect a seamless experience whether they're shopping from a desktop or their mobile phones. According to research, **mobile commerce** is growing rapidly, and a mobile-friendly website can directly impact sales.

Using Bootstrap or Custom CSS for Mobile-First Development

To build a responsive e-commerce site, you can either use a front-end framework like **Bootstrap** or write your own custom CSS. Both approaches are popular, but Bootstrap provides a quicker, more standardized way to implement responsive design features.

1. **Bootstrap for Mobile-First Development**: Bootstrap is a widely-used front-end framework that helps developers build responsive, mobile-first websites quickly. It includes pre-designed components and grid systems that adapt to different screen sizes. Bootstrap uses a mobile-

first approach, which means it designs the website for mobile devices first, then scales up for larger screens like tablets and desktops.

- o **Mobile-First Grid System**: Bootstrap uses a 12-column grid system to create layouts that scale to different devices. It also includes responsive classes like col-xs-12, col-sm-6, col-md-4, and col-lg-3 to control how elements are arranged on various screen sizes.

Example of Bootstrap Grid System:

html

```
<div class="container">
    <div class="row">
        <div    class="col-xs-12    col-sm-6
col-md-4 col-lg-3">
            <div class="product-card">
                <img      src="product.jpg"
alt="Product">
                <h4>Product Name</h4>
                <p>$199.99</p>
            </div>
        </div>
        <div    class="col-xs-12    col-sm-6
col-md-4 col-lg-3">
            <div class="product-card">
```

```
              <img      src="product2.jpg"
alt="Product">
              <h4>Product 2</h4>
              <p>$129.99</p>
          </div>
      </div>
      <!-- More products -->
  </div>
</div>
```

- o **Breakpoints**: Bootstrap's grid system automatically adjusts the layout based on the screen width. The `col-xs-12` class ensures full-width on extra small screens (phones), while the `col-md-4` class divides the grid into three columns on medium screens (tablets) and `col-lg-3` divides it into four columns on large screens (desktops).

- o **Responsive Navigation Bar**: One of the most common elements to adjust for mobile devices is the navigation bar. Bootstrap's navbar component automatically collapses into a hamburger menu on smaller screens.

Example of a Bootstrap Navbar:

```
html
```

```
<nav       class="navbar       navbar-expand-lg
navbar-light bg-light">
    <a                  class="navbar-brand"
href="#">YourStore</a>
    <button           class="navbar-toggler"
type="button" data-toggle="collapse" data-
target="#navbarNav"                    aria-
controls="navbarNav" aria-expanded="false"
aria-label="Toggle navigation">
        <span          class="navbar-toggler-
icon"></span>
    </button>
    <div class="collapse navbar-collapse"
id="navbarNav">
        <ul class="navbar-nav">
            <li class="nav-item active">
                <a          class="nav-link"
href="#">Home</a>
            </li>
            <li class="nav-item">
                <a          class="nav-link"
href="#">Shop</a>
            </li>
            <li class="nav-item">
                <a          class="nav-link"
href="#">Contact</a>
            </li>
        </ul>
    </div>
```

```
</nav>
```

- o **Mobile Navigation**: The hamburger menu (`navbar-toggler`) will appear on smaller screens, while the full navigation bar will be visible on larger screens.

2. **Custom CSS for Mobile-First Development**: If you prefer more control over the design or want a lightweight solution, you can write custom CSS to create a mobile-first design. This involves using **media queries** to apply different styles depending on the screen size.

- o **Basic Structure for Custom CSS**:

css

```css
/* Base styles for mobile devices (mobile-
first) */
body {
    font-family: Arial, sans-serif;
    padding: 10px;
}


.product-card {
    width: 100%;   /* Full width on mobile
*/
    margin-bottom: 20px;
}


/* Styles for tablets (600px and above) */
```

```
@media (min-width: 600px) {
    .product-card {
        width: 48%;   /* Two columns on
tablets */
        display: inline-block;
        margin-right: 4%;
    }
}


/* Styles for desktops (1024px and above)
*/
@media (min-width: 1024px) {
    .product-card {
        width: 23%;   /* Four columns on
desktops */
    }
}
```

- o **Media Queries**: The @media rule allows you to apply different styles based on the screen width. In this example, we use min-width to apply styles at specific breakpoints: 600px for tablets and 1024px for desktops. This way, the website adjusts as the screen size increases.

- o **Mobile-First Layout**: Notice that in the base styles (before the media queries), the .product-card is set to 100% width, meaning the products will be stacked vertically on mobile devices. For larger screens, the layout adapts with two columns on tablets and four columns on desktops.

Ensuring Your Store Works Across Different Screen Sizes

To ensure your e-commerce store works well across all devices, follow these best practices:

1. **Test Responsively**:
   o Use **responsive design testing tools** like Google Chrome's Developer Tools to simulate different screen sizes and check how your website behaves. You can toggle between different device views to test your layout.
   o Try testing on real devices as well (phones, tablets, desktops) to ensure that your store works across all platforms.

2. **Optimize Images for Mobile**:
   o Ensure that images are responsive and resize based on the screen size. You can use the `max-width: 100%` property to make images scale properly on smaller screens.

```css
css

img {
    max-width: 100%;
    height: auto;
```

}

- o **Use Image Compression**: Large images can slow down your website, especially on mobile devices. Use image compression techniques to reduce file sizes without compromising quality.

3. **Prioritize Mobile Performance**:
   - o Mobile users are often on slower networks, so optimize performance by reducing the number of HTTP requests and minifying your CSS, JavaScript, and HTML files.
   - o Use lazy loading for images and videos to only load content when it's needed (e.g., when it comes into the viewport).

4. **Mobile-Friendly Checkout**: The checkout process should be streamlined for mobile users. Make forms easy to fill out by using large input fields and providing auto-fill options for addresses and payment details. Additionally, ensure the "Proceed to Checkout" button is large and easy to tap on mobile devices.
   - o **Simplify Forms**: Use fewer fields on mobile and display only the most relevant information.
   - o **Large Touch Targets**: Buttons and links should be large enough to be tapped easily on small screens.

5. **Touchscreen-Friendly Features**: Many mobile users will be interacting with your site via touch. Ensure that all

clickable elements (e.g., buttons, links, and menus) are large enough to be tapped comfortably. This will reduce frustration for mobile users.

Conclusion

By the end of this chapter, you should have a solid understanding of how to build a **responsive design** for your e-commerce store. Whether you choose to use **Bootstrap** or **custom CSS**, the key is to ensure that your store is **mobile-first**, meaning it will look great and function well on mobile devices before scaling up to larger screens. A responsive e-commerce store is essential for providing an optimal shopping experience across all devices, leading to higher customer satisfaction and increased sales.

CHAPTER 13

ADDING SEARCH FUNCTIONALITY TO YOUR STORE

A search function is a crucial part of any e-commerce store. It allows customers to quickly find the products they are looking for, enhancing the user experience and potentially increasing conversions. In this chapter, we will cover how to implement a **basic search bar, filter search results by product attributes**, and use **full-text search with MySQL** for more complex and efficient querying.

Implementing a Basic Search Bar

The first step is to create a simple search bar where users can input their query. This search bar will allow users to search for products by name or description.

1. **Creating the Search Form**: The search bar will typically be placed in the header or sidebar of your website so users can access it easily. Here's a simple form for the search bar:

File: /products/search-form.php:

php

```
<form      method="GET"      action="search-
results.php">
    <input     type="text"     name="query"
placeholder="Search products..." required>
    <button type="submit">Search</button>
</form>
```

- o **Form Method**: The form uses the GET method, which appends the search query to the URL as a query parameter (query). This makes it easy to link directly to search results.
- o **Placeholder**: The placeholder text encourages users to search for products by name or other attributes.

2. **Handling the Search Query**: When the user submits the search form, we need to retrieve the query parameter and use it to search for products in the database.

File: /products/search-results.php:

php

```
<?php
session_start();
include '../config/db.php';
```

147

```php
if (isset($_GET['query'])) {
    $search_query = $_GET['query'];

    // SQL query to search for products by
name or description
    $sql = "SELECT * FROM products WHERE
name LIKE ? OR description LIKE ?";
    $stmt = $conn->prepare($sql);
    $search_term = "%" . $search_query .
"%";
    $stmt->bind_param("ss", $search_term,
$search_term);
    $stmt->execute();
    $result = $stmt->get_result();

    if ($result->num_rows > 0) {
        echo "<h2>Search Results for
'$search_query'</h2>";
        echo "<div class='product-list'>";
        while ($product = $result-
>fetch_assoc()) {
            echo "<div class='product'>";
            echo "<h3>" . $product['name']
. "</h3>";
            echo "<p>" .
$product['description'] . "</p>";
            echo "<p>Price: $" .
$product['price'] . "</p>";
```

```
            echo      "<a      href='product-
details.php?id="  .  $product['product_id']
. "'>View Details</a>";
            echo "</div>";
        }
        echo "</div>";
    } else {
        echo   "No   products   found   for
'$search_query'.";
    }
}
?>
```

- o **Searching the Database**: The SQL query uses LIKE to match the query input with the name or description fields in the products table.
- o **Displaying Results**: If products are found, they are displayed in a loop. Each product's name, description, price, and a link to its detailed page are shown.
- o **No Results**: If no products are found, a message is displayed informing the user that no results were found.

Filtering Search Results by Product Attributes

In addition to a basic search, customers often want to filter their search results by product attributes such as price range, category, or brand. We can add filtering options to refine the search results.

1. **Adding Filter Options**: You can provide filters based on product categories, price range, and other attributes. Here's how you can modify the search form to include filters.

   File: /products/search-form.php (updated with filters):

   php

   ```
   <form     method="GET"     action="search-
   results.php">
       <input    type="text"    name="query"
   placeholder="Search products..." required>

       <label
   for="category">Category:</label>
       <select name="category">
           <option              value="">All
   Categories</option>
           <?php
           // Fetch categories from the
   database
   ```

```php
$sql = "SELECT * FROM categories";
$result = $conn->query($sql);
while ($category = $result->fetch_assoc()) {
    echo "<option value='" . $category['category_id'] . "'>" . $category['name'] . "</option>";
}
?>
</select>

<label for="min_price">Min Price:</label>
<input type="number" name="min_price" placeholder="0" step="0.01">

<label for="max_price">Max Price:</label>
<input type="number" name="max_price" placeholder="1000" step="0.01">

<button type="submit">Search</button>
</form>
```

- o **Category Filter**: This dropdown allows users to filter products by category.
- o **Price Range**: Two input fields allow users to filter by minimum and maximum price.

    o **Action**: The form submits the search query along with the selected filter options to the `search-results.php` page.

2. **Handling Filtered Search Results**: In the `search-results.php` file, you can modify the query to apply the selected filters.

File: `/products/search-results.php` (updated with filters):

php

```php
<?php
session_start();
include '../config/db.php';

if (isset($_GET['query'])) {
    $search_query = $_GET['query'];
    $category_id = $_GET['category'] ??
'';
    $min_price = $_GET['min_price'] ?? 0;
    $max_price = $_GET['max_price'] ??
10000;

    // Build the SQL query with filters
    $sql = "SELECT * FROM products WHERE
(name LIKE ? OR description LIKE ?)";

    if ($category_id) {
```

152

```php
        $sql .= " AND category_id = ?";
    }
    if ($min_price) {
        $sql .= " AND price >= ?";
    }
    if ($max_price) {
        $sql .= " AND price <= ?";
    }


    $stmt = $conn->prepare($sql);
    $search_term = "%" . $search_query . "%";
    $params        =        [$search_term, $search_term];

    if ($category_id) {
        $params[] = $category_id;
    }
    if ($min_price) {
        $params[] = $min_price;
    }
    if ($max_price) {
        $params[] = $max_price;
    }

    $stmt->bind_param(str_repeat("s", count($params)), ...$params);
    $stmt->execute();
    $result = $stmt->get_result();
```

153

```php
    if ($result->num_rows > 0) {
        echo "<h2>Search Results for
'$search_query'</h2>";
        echo "<div class='product-list'>";
        while ($product = $result-
>fetch_assoc()) {
            echo "<div class='product'>";
            echo "<h3>" . $product['name']
. "</h3>";
            echo "<p>" .
$product['description'] . "</p>";
            echo "<p>Price: $" .
$product['price'] . "</p>";
            echo "<a href='product-
details.php?id=" . $product['product_id']
. "'>View Details</a>";
            echo "</div>";
        }
        echo "</div>";
    } else {
        echo "No products found for
'$search_query'.";
    }
}
?>
```

- o **SQL Query with Filters**: The SQL query dynamically adds conditions for category and

154

price range based on the user's input. If no filter is selected, the query searches across all products.

- o **Binding Parameters**: We use `bind_param` to bind the dynamic parameters (search query, category ID, price range) to the SQL statement securely.

Using Full-Text Search with MySQL for More Complex Queries

While `LIKE` queries are simple and useful for basic search, they can become inefficient as the database grows. **Full-text search** in MySQL allows for more complex and efficient queries, particularly when you want to search large amounts of text (such as product descriptions) more effectively.

1. **Enabling Full-Text Index**: First, ensure that your `products` table has a **full-text index** on the `name` and `description` columns. This index speeds up text searches significantly.

```sql
ALTER TABLE products ADD FULLTEXT(name, description);
```

2. **Using Full-Text Search in Queries**: MySQL provides the `MATCH ... AGAINST` syntax for full-text searching.

This allows for more flexible and advanced searches, including natural language search and boolean search.

Example Full-Text Search Query:

```sql
SELECT * FROM products WHERE MATCH(name,
description) AGAINST('search term' IN
NATURAL LANGUAGE MODE);
```

- o **IN NATURAL LANGUAGE MODE**: This option allows for a more flexible search, ranking results based on relevance to the search term.

3. **Using Full-Text Search in PHP**: You can integrate full-text search into your search functionality. Here's how you can modify the `search-results.php` file to use `MATCH ... AGAINST`:

File: /products/search-results.php (using full-text search):

```php
<?php
session_start();
include '../config/db.php';

if (isset($_GET['query'])) {
```

```php
$search_query = $_GET['query'];

// Full-text search query
$sql = "SELECT * FROM products WHERE
MATCH(name, description) AGAINST(?)";
$stmt = $conn->prepare($sql);
$stmt->bind_param("s", $search_query);
$stmt->execute();
$result = $stmt->get_result();

if ($result->num_rows > 0) {
    echo "<h2>Search Results for
'$search_query'</h2>";
        echo "<div class='product-list'>";
        while ($product = $result-
>fetch_assoc()) {
            echo "<div class='product'>";
            echo "<h3>" . $product['name']
. "</h3>";
            echo         "<p>"         .
$product['description'] . "</p>";
            echo     "<p>Price:     $"     .
$product['price'] . "</p>";
            echo     "<a     href='product-
details.php?id=" . $product['product_id']
. "'>View Details</a>";
            echo "</div>";
        }
        echo "</div>";
```

```
    } else {
        echo    "No    products    found    for
'$search_query'.";
    }
}
?>
```

- o **Full-Text Search Query**: The query uses MATCH and AGAINST to search for the term in both the product name and description.

Conclusion

By the end of this chapter, you should have a fully functional **search system** for your e-commerce store. You learned how to implement a basic search bar, filter search results by product attributes, and use **full-text search** in MySQL for more advanced and efficient queries. With these features, your customers can easily find the products they are looking for, improving the overall user experience and increasing the chances of conversions.

CHAPTER 14

IMPLEMENTING USER REVIEWS AND RATINGS

User reviews and ratings play a significant role in an e-commerce store by providing valuable feedback for other customers and enhancing trust in your products. In this chapter, we will implement a **review and rating system** that allows customers to review products, display average ratings, and manage review moderation to ensure the quality of feedback.

Allowing Customers to Review Products

To enable customers to review products, we need a system where they can leave feedback and rate products on a scale (e.g., 1 to 5 stars). Reviews typically include a rating, a comment, and the user's information.

1. **Creating the Reviews Table**: First, you need to create a database table to store the product reviews. The `reviews` table should link each review to a specific product and user.

   Example SQL query to create the `reviews` table:

```sql
sql


CREATE TABLE reviews (
    review_id INT AUTO_INCREMENT PRIMARY KEY,
    product_id INT NOT NULL,
    user_id INT NOT NULL,
    rating INT NOT NULL,
    comment TEXT,
    review_date TIMESTAMP DEFAULT CURRENT_TIMESTAMP,
    FOREIGN KEY (product_id) REFERENCES products(product_id),
    FOREIGN KEY (user_id) REFERENCES users(user_id)
);
```

- o   `review_id`: A unique identifier for each review.
- o   `product_id`: A foreign key linking to the `products` table.
- o   `user_id`: A foreign key linking to the `users` table to identify the reviewer.
- o   `rating`: The star rating (usually between 1 and 5).
- o   `comment`: The textual review provided by the customer.
- o   `review_date`: Timestamp for when the review was submitted.

160

2. **Allowing Customers to Submit Reviews**: Next, create a form where users can submit reviews and ratings for products. The form will capture the product ID, the user's rating, and a comment.

File: /products/review-form.php (for submitting reviews):

php

```php
<?php
session_start();
if (!isset($_SESSION['user_id'])) {
    echo "Please log in to leave a review.";
    exit();
}

if (isset($_GET['product_id'])) {
    $product_id = $_GET['product_id'];
}
?>

<h3>Leave a Review</h3>
<form method="POST" action="submit-review.php?product_id=<?php echo $product_id; ?>">
    <label for="rating">Rating (1 to 5):</label>
```

```
<input      type="number"      name="rating"
min="1" max="5" required><br>

<label for="comment">Comment:</label>
<textarea                   name="comment"
required></textarea><br>

<button                        type="submit"
name="submit_review">Submit
Review</button>
</form>
```

- o **Rating**: The user provides a rating between 1 and 5.
- o **Comment**: The user can leave a comment about the product.
- o **Action**: The form submits the data to the submit-review.php script.

3. **Processing Review Submissions**: In the submit-review.php script, you'll process the form data and insert the review into the database.

File: /products/submit-review.php:

php

```
<?php
session_start();
include '../config/db.php';
```

```php
if (!isset($_SESSION['user_id'])) {
    echo "Please log in to leave a review.";
    exit();
}

if (isset($_POST['submit_review'])) {
    $user_id = $_SESSION['user_id'];
    $product_id = $_GET['product_id'];
    $rating = $_POST['rating'];
    $comment = $_POST['comment'];

    // Insert the review into the reviews table
    $sql = "INSERT INTO reviews (product_id, user_id, rating, comment) VALUES (?, ?, ?, ?)";
    $stmt = $conn->prepare($sql);
    $stmt->bind_param("iiis", $product_id, $user_id, $rating, $comment);
    if ($stmt->execute()) {
        echo "Review submitted successfully!";
    } else {
        echo "Error: " . $stmt->error;
    }
}
?>
```

o **Inserting the Review**: The review details are inserted into the `reviews` table, including the product ID, user ID, rating, and comment.

Displaying Average Ratings and Review Counts

To give potential customers an idea of how well a product is rated, it's important to show the **average rating** and **total number of reviews** on the product page.

1. **Calculating Average Rating**: To display the average rating, you can calculate it by averaging the `rating` column from the `reviews` table for each product.

   SQL Query for Average Rating:

   ```sql
   sql

   SELECT   AVG(rating)   AS   average_rating,
   COUNT(review_id) AS review_count
   FROM reviews WHERE product_id = ?;
   ```

2. **Displaying the Average Rating and Review Count**: In the product details page, fetch the average rating and total review count from the database and display it.

   File: /products/product-details.php:

   ```php
   php
   ```

```php
<?php
session_start();
include '../config/db.php';

if (isset($_GET['product_id'])) {
    $product_id = $_GET['product_id'];

    // Fetch the average rating and review
count
    $sql = "SELECT AVG(rating) AS
average_rating, COUNT(review_id) AS
review_count FROM reviews WHERE product_id
= ?";
    $stmt = $conn->prepare($sql);
    $stmt->bind_param("i", $product_id);
    $stmt->execute();
    $result = $stmt->get_result();
    $review_data = $result->fetch_assoc();

    $average_rating =
round($review_data['average_rating'], 1);
    $review_count =
$review_data['review_count'];

    echo "<h3>Product Rating</h3>";
    echo "<p>Average Rating: " .
($average_rating ? $average_rating : "No
ratings yet") . " / 5</p>";
```

165

```
echo     "<p>Total     Reviews:     "    .
$review_count . "</p>";
}
?>
```

- o **Displaying Ratings**: The average rating is rounded to one decimal place, and if there are no reviews, a message indicates that there are no ratings yet.
- o **Review Count**: The total number of reviews for the product is displayed.

Moderating Reviews and Dealing with Spam

User reviews can sometimes be misused or contain inappropriate content. It's essential to implement a moderation system to ensure the quality of reviews on your site.

1. **Moderating Reviews**: You can add an `is_approved` column to the `reviews` table to flag reviews that are pending approval before they appear on the site.

   Modify the `reviews` table to include the `is_approved` column:

   sql

   ```sql
   ALTER TABLE reviews ADD COLUMN is_approved
   BOOLEAN DEFAULT FALSE;
   ```

166

2. **Admin Panel for Moderating Reviews**: Admins can review all submitted reviews and approve or reject them before they appear on the product page.

   File: /admin/moderate-reviews.php:

   php

```php
<?php
session_start();
if ($_SESSION['user_role'] !== 'admin') {
    header("Location: login.php");
    exit();
}

include '../config/db.php';

// Fetch all unapproved reviews
$sql = "SELECT r.review_id, r.product_id,
r.rating, r.comment, r.is_approved, p.name
FROM reviews r JOIN products p ON
r.product_id = p.product_id WHERE
r.is_approved = FALSE";
$result = $conn->query($sql);

echo "<h2>Pending Reviews</h2>";
while ($review = $result->fetch_assoc()) {
    echo "<p>Product: " . $review['name']
. "<br>";
```

```php
    echo "Rating: " . $review['rating'] .
"/5<br>";
    echo "Comment: " . $review['comment']
. "<br>";
    echo "<a href='approve-review.php?id="
. $review['review_id'] . "'>Approve</a> |
<a      href='reject-review.php?id="      .
$review['review_id'] . "'>Reject</a></p>";
}
?>
```

- o **Displaying Pending Reviews**: The admin can view all unapproved reviews. They can either approve or reject each review.

3. **Approve/Reject Review**: The admin can approve or reject reviews by changing the is_approved column in the reviews table.

File: /admin/approve-review.php:

php

```php
<?php
session_start();
if ($_SESSION['user_role'] !== 'admin') {
    header("Location: login.php");
    exit();
}
```

```php
include '../config/db.php';

if (isset($_GET['id'])) {
    $review_id = $_GET['id'];

    // Update the review status to approved
    $sql = "UPDATE reviews SET is_approved
= TRUE WHERE review_id = ?";
    $stmt = $conn->prepare($sql);
    $stmt->bind_param("i", $review_id);
    if ($stmt->execute()) {
        echo "Review approved!";
    } else {
        echo "Error: " . $stmt->error;
    }
}
?>
```

- o **Approve**: The admin can approve a review by setting is_approved to TRUE, allowing it to appear on the product page.

4. **Dealing with Spam**: To combat spam or inappropriate reviews, you can implement features like:

   - o **Word filters**: Check reviews for certain keywords or phrases and flag them as potentially inappropriate.

o **CAPTCHA**: Add a CAPTCHA to the review submission form to prevent automated spam submissions.

o **Flagging System**: Allow users to report inappropriate reviews.

For example, you can add a simple word filter to reject reviews with certain keywords:

php

```php
$banned_words = ["spam", "fake", "inappropriate"];
foreach ($banned_words as $word) {
    if (strpos(strtolower($comment), $word) !== false) {
        echo "Review contains inappropriate content.";
        exit();
    }
}
```

Conclusion

By the end of this chapter, you will have a fully functional **review and rating system** for your e-commerce store. Customers can leave reviews, rate products, and view average ratings and review counts. You will also have implemented **moderation** to ensure the quality of reviews, including the ability to approve or reject reviews, and manage spam. This system will help you build trust with your customers and improve the overall shopping experience.

CHAPTER 15

OPTIMIZING FOR SEO

Search Engine Optimization (SEO) is crucial for driving organic traffic to your e-commerce site. Proper SEO practices increase your site's visibility in search engine results, making it easier for potential customers to find your products. In this chapter, we will cover the basics of SEO for e-commerce, focusing on meta tags, URL structure, image alt attributes, and strategies to ensure your site ranks well for product searches.

Understanding Basic SEO Concepts for E-Commerce

SEO involves optimizing various aspects of your website to improve its ranking in search engine results pages (SERPs). For e-commerce sites, SEO focuses on ensuring that your products, categories, and content are easily discoverable by search engines. The key components of SEO include:

1. **On-Page SEO**: Optimizing the content on your website, including product descriptions, images, and meta tags.
2. **Technical SEO**: Ensuring that your website is technically optimized for search engines, including site speed, mobile-friendliness, and URL structure.

172

3. **Off-Page SEO**: Building backlinks and social signals that improve the authority of your site in the eyes of search engines.

4. **Local SEO**: If you have a physical store or serve specific regions, local SEO optimizes your presence in local search results.

For e-commerce sites, the most important on-page SEO strategies include optimizing product pages, category pages, and ensuring a clean URL structure.

Using Meta Tags, URL Structure, and Alt Attributes

1. **Meta Tags**: Meta tags provide information about a webpage that helps search engines understand the content. The most important meta tags for e-commerce SEO are the **title tag**, **meta description**, and **meta robots tag**.

    o **Title Tag**: This is the title of the page that appears in search results. It should include relevant keywords for the product or category. The title tag should be concise and describe the content of the page.

    Example:

    ```
    html
    ```

```
<title>Organic Cotton T-Shirts -
Eco-Friendly Fashion |
YourStore</title>
```

- Keep it under 60 characters.
- Include important keywords (e.g., product type, brand, and other relevant terms).

o **Meta Description**: The meta description provides a brief summary of the page's content and appears under the title in search results. While it doesn't directly impact rankings, it influences the click-through rate (CTR).

Example:

html

```
<meta name="description"
content="Shop our collection of
organic cotton t-shirts.
Comfortable, stylish, and eco-
friendly. Available in various
colors and sizes. Free shipping on
orders over $50.">
```

- Keep it under 160 characters.
- Include a call-to-action (CTA), such as "Shop now" or "Buy today."

o **Meta Robots Tag**: This tag controls how search engines index the page. For product pages and category pages, you should allow search engines to index and follow the links.

Example:

```
html
```

```
<meta name="robots" content="index,
follow">
```

2. **URL Structure**: A clean and descriptive URL structure is essential for both search engines and users. Use short, keyword-rich URLs that are easy to read and understand. Ideally, your URLs should reflect the content of the page.

   o **Use Keywords in URLs**: Include relevant keywords for the product, category, or page.

   o **Use Hyphens, Not Underscores**: Use hyphens (–) to separate words in URLs, as search engines treat hyphens as space, but underscores are ignored.

Example of a product URL:

```
plaintext
```

```
https://www.yourstore.com/products/organi
c-cotton-t-shirt
```

Example of a category URL:

```
plaintext
```

```
https://www.yourstore.com/categories/eco-
friendly-fashion
```

- o **Avoid Long and Complex URLs**: Keep URLs short and simple. Avoid including unnecessary parameters or session IDs in the URL.

3. **Image Alt Attributes**: Images are an essential part of e-commerce websites, but search engines can't "see" images. The `alt` attribute provides a textual description of an image, helping search engines index the image properly. It also enhances accessibility for visually impaired users.

   - o **Descriptive Alt Text**: Use descriptive and relevant alt text for every image, especially for product images. Include keywords when appropriate, but avoid keyword stuffing.

   Example:

   ```
   html
   ```

```
<img          src="organic-cotton-t-
shirt.jpg"  alt="Organic  Cotton    T-
Shirt for Men in Blue">
```

- o **For Product Images**: Include details like product type, color, and features.
- o **For Category Images**: Include the category name and relevant terms.

Ensuring Your Site Ranks Well for Product Searches

1. **Optimizing Product Descriptions**: Product descriptions are key to both user experience and SEO. Write unique, engaging, and informative descriptions for each product. Include relevant keywords naturally, but avoid keyword stuffing.

   - o **Include Key Features**: Describe the product's key features (e.g., material, dimensions, color).
   - o **Use Bullet Points**: Use bullet points for easy readability, especially for important details like size, color, and special features.
   - o **Avoid Duplicate Content**: Make sure each product has a unique description. Avoid ing manufacturer descriptions verbatim.

Example:

```
html
```

```
<h1>Organic Cotton T-Shirt - Eco-Friendly
and Comfortable</h1>
<p>This organic cotton t-shirt is made from
100% sustainable materials, offering both
style and comfort. Available in a variety
of colors and sizes. Perfect for casual
wear or outdoor activities.</p>
<ul>
    <li>Material: 100% Organic Cotton</li>
    <li>Color: Available in Blue, Green,
and White</li>
    <li>Size:    Small,    Medium,    Large,
XL</li>
    <li>Machine washable</li>
</ul>
```

2. **Optimizing Product Images**: Product images play an essential role in both user experience and SEO. Large image files can slow down your website, which negatively impacts SEO rankings. Ensure that your product images are optimized for speed.

   o **Image Compression**: Use image compression tools to reduce the file size without compromising quality.

   o **Responsive Images**: Use the srcset attribute to provide different image sizes for different screen resolutions and devices.

Example:

```
html
```

```
<img src="product-small.jpg"
    srcset="product-large.jpg
1024w,    product-medium.jpg    768w,
product-small.jpg 320w"
    alt="Organic Cotton T-Shirt in
Blue" />
```

3. **Mobile Optimization**: With the growing number of mobile users, mobile optimization is crucial for both user experience and SEO. Google prioritizes mobile-friendly websites in its search rankings.

   o **Responsive Design**: Ensure your site is mobile-friendly and adapts to different screen sizes.

   o **Mobile Page Speed**: Optimize images and scripts to ensure fast loading times on mobile devices.

4. **Internal Linking and Breadcrumbs**: Internal linking helps search engines crawl your site and discover new content. It also improves user navigation. Implement **breadcrumbs** to create a logical and easily accessible navigation structure for both users and search engines.

Example:

```
html
```

```
<nav aria-label="breadcrumb">
    <ol class="breadcrumb">
        <li        class="breadcrumb-item"><a
href="/">Home</a></li>
        <li        class="breadcrumb-item"><a
href="/categories/eco-friendly-
fashion">Eco-Friendly Fashion</a></li>
        <li class="breadcrumb-item active"
aria-current="page">Organic    Cotton    T-
Shirt</li>
    </ol>
</nav>
```

- o **Link to Relevant Products**: Link related products and categories within product pages to improve SEO and user experience.
- o **Anchor Text**: Use descriptive anchor text when linking to other pages.

5. **User Reviews and Content**: **User-generated content**, such as reviews, adds fresh and relevant content to your product pages. Reviews often contain keywords that improve SEO and provide valuable content for search engines.

- o **Encourage Reviews**: Ask your customers to leave reviews for the products they've purchased. This helps improve content richness and SEO.

o **Display Average Ratings**: Show product ratings on search results pages and product pages. This can increase click-through rates (CTR) from search engine results.

6. **Optimizing Product Pages for Rich Snippets**: **Rich snippets** are enhanced search results that show additional information, such as star ratings, prices, and availability. Implement structured data (JSON-LD or Microdata) to enable rich snippets for your product pages.

Example of product schema using JSON-LD:

```json
json

{
    "@context": "http://schema.org",
    "@type": "Product",
    "name": "Organic Cotton T-Shirt",
    "image":
"https://www.yourstore.com/images/product
.jpg",
    "description": "A comfortable and eco-
friendly t-shirt made from 100% organic
cotton.",
    "sku": "12345",
    "offers": {
      "@type": "Offer",
```

```
    "url":
"https://www.yourstore.com/products/organ
ic-cotton-t-shirt",
    "priceCurrency": "USD",
    "price": "19.99",
    "priceValidUntil": "2025-12-31",
    "itemCondition":
"http://schema.org/NewCondition",
    "availability":
"http://schema.org/InStock",
    "seller": {
      "@type": "Organization",
      "name": "YourStore"
    }
  }
}
```

- o **Rich Snippets**: Implementing schema markup helps search engines display additional product details, which can enhance visibility and increase click-through rates.

Conclusion

By the end of this chapter, you should have a solid understanding of how to **optimize your e-commerce site for SEO**. You've learned how to implement meta tags, structure URLs effectively, optimize images with alt attributes, and ensure your site ranks well for product searches. With these SEO strategies in place, you can drive more organic traffic to your store, increase visibility in search engine results, and ultimately boost sales. SEO is an ongoing process, so continue to monitor your rankings and make adjustments as needed.

CHAPTER 16

SECURITY BEST PRACTICES FOR E-COMMERCE SITES

Security is a top priority for any e-commerce site, as it involves handling sensitive customer data, including payment information, personal details, and order histories. A breach can damage your reputation, lead to financial losses, and compromise customer trust. In this chapter, we will explore how to secure your e-commerce site by protecting it against common vulnerabilities, using HTTPS, and ensuring customer data safety through encryption.

Securing Your PHP Code Against Common Vulnerabilities

When developing a PHP-based e-commerce store, there are several security vulnerabilities to be aware of. We will cover three of the most common ones: **SQL Injection (SQLi)**, **Cross-Site Scripting (XSS)**, and **Cross-Site Request Forgery (CSRF)**, and provide best practices for mitigating them.

1. SQL Injection (SQLi)

SQL Injection is a security vulnerability where an attacker can manipulate a website's database query by inserting malicious SQL code into input fields (such as search bars or login forms). If you don't properly validate and sanitize user inputs, attackers can exploit this to gain unauthorized access to your database.

How to Prevent SQL Injection:

- **Use Prepared Statements (with Bind Parameters)**: In PHP, always use prepared statements with parameterized queries to separate SQL logic from user input. This makes it impossible for attackers to inject malicious SQL code.

Example:

```php
php

// Using prepared statements with MySQLi
$conn = new mysqli($host, $user, $password,
$dbname);

if ($conn->connect_error) {
    die("Connection failed: " . $conn-
>connect_error);
}

// Using prepared statement to prevent SQL
injection
$stmt = $conn->prepare("SELECT * FROM
products WHERE product_id = ?");
```

```
$stmt->bind_param("i",    $product_id);    //
'i' stands for integer
$stmt->execute();
$result = $stmt->get_result();

// Fetch results and process...
```

- o The `prepare` method ensures that the user input is treated as a value, not as part of the SQL query.
- o **Always validate and sanitize input**: While prepared statements are the primary defense, validating inputs (such as ensuring they are the correct data type) is also important.

2. Cross-Site Scripting (XSS)

Cross-Site Scripting (XSS) occurs when an attacker injects malicious scripts (usually JavaScript) into a website that other users then execute in their browsers. This can lead to session hijacking, defacement, or theft of sensitive information.

How to Prevent XSS:

- **Escape Output**: Whenever you output user-generated content (e.g., from form submissions or database results), make sure to escape special characters like <, >, and &, so they are displayed as text, not executed as code.

186

Example of escaping output:

```php
php
```

```php
echo          htmlspecialchars($user_input,
ENT_QUOTES, 'UTF-8');
```

- o htmlspecialchars() converts special characters to HTML entities, which prevents the browser from interpreting them as executable code.
- **Use Content Security Policy (CSP)**: CSP is a browser feature that can help prevent XSS attacks by controlling which content (scripts, stylesheets, images, etc.) can be loaded and executed.

Example of adding a CSP header:

```php
php
```

```php
header("Content-Security-Policy: default-
src 'self'; script-src 'self';");
```

- o This ensures that only scripts from the same origin as the site are executed, preventing third-party scripts from running.

3. Cross-Site Request Forgery (CSRF)

CSRF is an attack that tricks the user into making an unwanted request (such as submitting a form) without their knowledge or consent. For example, an attacker might send a link to a user that causes them to transfer money or change account settings.

How to Prevent CSRF:

- **Use Anti-CSRF Tokens**: Generate a unique token for every form submission, and ensure that the token is checked when the form is submitted. This ensures that the request is legitimate and not forged.

  Example:

  php

  ```php
  // Generate a token when the form is displayed
  $_SESSION['csrf_token'] = bin2hex(random_bytes(32));

  // Add the token to the form
  echo '<input type="hidden" name="csrf_token" value="' . $_SESSION['csrf_token'] . '">';
  ```

- o When the form is submitted, check the token to ensure it matches the one stored in the session.

```php
if          ($_POST['csrf_token']          !==
$_SESSION['csrf_token']) {
    die("Invalid CSRF token");
}
```

- o This ensures that the form submission is coming from your own website and not an attacker.

Using HTTPS and SSL Certificates

HTTPS (Hypertext Transfer Protocol Secure) is essential for protecting sensitive data, especially when users enter payment information or personal details. HTTPS encrypts the connection between the user's browser and your server, ensuring that any data sent or received is secure.

1. **Obtain an SSL Certificate**: An **SSL certificate** encrypts the data between the server and the user. It also provides authentication, ensuring that users are connecting to the correct website and not a malicious version.
   - o You can obtain an SSL certificate from a trusted Certificate Authority (CA), or use services like Let's Encrypt, which offers free SSL certificates.

189

2. **Enforce HTTPS**: Ensure your website always uses HTTPS by configuring your server to redirect HTTP traffic to HTTPS.

Example of enforcing HTTPS in `.htaccess` (Apache):

apache

```
RewriteEngine On
RewriteCond %{HTTPS} off
RewriteRule                              ^
https://%{HTTP_HOST}%{REQUEST_URI}
[L,R=301]
```

3. **Use Strong Cipher Suites**: Make sure to use strong encryption protocols such as TLS 1.2 or TLS 1.3, and disable outdated protocols like SSL 3.0 and TLS 1.0 to ensure the highest level of encryption.

4. **HSTS (HTTP Strict Transport Security)**: Use **HSTS** to enforce the use of HTTPS. It instructs browsers to always connect using HTTPS, even if the user tries to visit an HTTP version of your site.

Example of adding HSTS in `.htaccess`:

apache

```
Header   always   set   Strict-Transport-
Security                "max-age=31536000;
includeSubDomains"
```

Keeping Customer Data Safe with Encryption

E-commerce websites handle sensitive data, including customer details, payment information, and order histories. Protecting this data is vital for maintaining trust and complying with regulations like GDPR or PCI DSS.

1. **Encrypting Sensitive Data**: When storing sensitive customer information, such as passwords or credit card details, always use encryption techniques to protect it. Never store sensitive data in plain text.

   o **Passwords**: Use strong hashing algorithms like **bcrypt** or **Argon2** to hash passwords before storing them in your database. These algorithms are designed to be computationally expensive, which makes them resistant to brute-force attacks.

   Example of hashing a password using bcrypt in PHP:

   ```php
   php
   ```

191

```
$hashed_password                    =
password_hash($password,
PASSWORD_BCRYPT);
```

o **Encryption for Sensitive Data**: For other sensitive data (e.g., credit card numbers, personal information), use **AES-256 encryption** to store it securely.

Example of encrypting and decrypting data using AES-256 in PHP:

```php
php

$key = 'your-secret-key';
$data = 'Sensitive data to encrypt';

// Encrypt data
$encrypted_data                     =
openssl_encrypt($data,       'aes-256-
cbc', $key, 0, $iv);

// Decrypt data
$decrypted_data                     =
openssl_decrypt($encrypted_data,
'aes-256-cbc', $key, 0, $iv);
```

2. **Secure Payment Processing**: When handling payments, **never store full credit card information**. Use secure,

192

PCI-compliant third-party payment processors like **Stripe** or **PayPal** to handle transactions. These services encrypt and securely process payment data, so you don't have to store sensitive information on your server.

3. **Tokenization**: Tokenization is the process of replacing sensitive data with a unique identifier, or "token," which can be used for future transactions without exposing the original data. This is a common technique used in payment processing systems.

4. **Secure Database Access**:

   o Always use **least privilege** when granting database access. Ensure that only the necessary users and services have access to sensitive data.

   o Use **firewalls** and **SQL security** settings to restrict access to the database.

Conclusion

By the end of this chapter, you should have a clear understanding of the best practices to secure your e-commerce site and protect customer data. Here are the key takeaways:

1. **Protect against common vulnerabilities** such as **SQL injection**, **XSS**, and **CSRF** by using prepared statements, escaping output, and employing anti-CSRF tokens.

2. **Enforce HTTPS** across your entire site with SSL certificates, strong cipher suites, and HSTS.

3. **Encrypt sensitive customer data** using techniques like **bcrypt** for password storage and **AES-256** for other types of sensitive data.

4. **Use trusted third-party services** for payment processing to avoid storing sensitive financial information on your servers.

Security is an ongoing process, so make sure to regularly audit your website, update software, and stay informed about the latest security practices to keep your e-commerce site safe and trustworthy.

CHAPTER 17

IMPLEMENTING SHIPPING AND TAX CALCULATION

Shipping and tax calculation are critical aspects of any e-commerce platform. Offering accurate and flexible shipping options, along with proper tax calculations based on the customer's location, ensures a smooth checkout process and a better customer experience. In this chapter, we will cover how to implement different **shipping options**, calculate **taxes based on location**, and integrate with **shipping providers** like FedEx, UPS, and others.

Creating Different Shipping Options (Flat Rate, By Weight, etc.)

Shipping options depend on the product's size, weight, destination, and sometimes other factors like urgency or special handling. We will implement different types of shipping methods to cater to different business models.

1. Flat Rate Shipping

Flat-rate shipping charges a fixed amount for all orders, regardless of the product's weight, size, or destination. This is a simple and predictable option for customers.

- **Implementation**: To implement flat-rate shipping, you simply add a fixed cost to the order, which can be configured in the system's settings or database.

Example of Flat Rate Shipping in PHP:

php

```php
$flat_rate_shipping = 5.00;   // Flat rate
cost

// Add flat rate shipping to total order
cost
$total_order_cost = $total_product_cost +
$flat_rate_shipping;
```

- **Considerations**: Flat-rate shipping works best for smaller or uniform-sized products, but it may not be cost-effective for businesses with large or varied product sizes.

2. Shipping by Weight

With shipping by weight, the shipping cost is calculated based on the weight of the products in the order. This method is commonly used by businesses that sell products of varying sizes and weights.

- **Implementation**: Calculate the total weight of the products in the cart and multiply it by a predefined rate.

Example of Shipping by Weight in PHP:

```php
php

$shipping_rate_per_kg = 2.00;  // Cost per
kg
$total_weight = 0;

// Calculate the total weight of the
products in the cart
foreach ($_SESSION['cart'] as $item) {
    $total_weight += $item['weight'] *
$item['quantity'];  // weight in kg
}

// Calculate the shipping cost
$shipping_cost = $total_weight *
$shipping_rate_per_kg;

// Add shipping cost to the total order
cost
$total_order_cost = $total_product_cost +
$shipping_cost;
```

- **Considerations**: Shipping by weight works well for businesses with products of different weights and sizes. It's more accurate than flat-rate shipping, but it can be complex to manage.

3. Shipping by Price

Some stores may charge shipping based on the total value of the order. Higher-value orders might qualify for free or discounted shipping.

- **Implementation**: Define shipping costs based on different order price ranges.

   Example of Shipping by Price in PHP:

   php

```php
if ($total_product_cost < 50) {
    $shipping_cost = 10.00;   // Standard
shipping cost for orders under $50
} elseif ($total_product_cost >= 50 &&
$total_product_cost < 100) {
    $shipping_cost = 5.00;   // Discounted
shipping for orders between $50 and $100
} else {
    $shipping_cost = 0.00;   // Free
shipping for orders over $100
}


// Add shipping cost to the total order
cost
$total_order_cost = $total_product_cost +
$shipping_cost;
```

- **Considerations**: This method is simple but works best for businesses that want to incentivize larger purchases. It can also be used in combination with other methods like flat-rate or weight-based shipping.

Calculating Taxes Based on the User's Location

Tax rates vary by country, state, region, and even city. In order to calculate taxes accurately, you need to know the customer's location and apply the appropriate tax rate.

1. Basic Tax Calculation

To calculate taxes, you first need to know the customer's location, specifically the country and, optionally, the state or region. You can either ask the user to enter their location during checkout or use their IP address to estimate their location.

- **Example of Tax Calculation in PHP**:

```php
$tax_rate = 0.07;   // Default tax rate of
7%

// If the user is in a specific state or
region, adjust the tax rate
if      ($_SESSION['user_location']      ==
'California') {
```

```
    $tax_rate = 0.075;   // Higher tax rate
for California
} elseif ($_SESSION['user_location'] ==
'New York') {
    $tax_rate = 0.08;   // Tax rate for New
York
}

// Calculate the tax amount
$tax_amount   =   $total_product_cost   *
$tax_rate;

// Add tax to the total order cost
$total_order_cost = $total_product_cost +
$tax_amount;
```

2. Using Tax APIs for Automatic Tax Calculation

For more accurate and dynamic tax calculation, consider integrating with a tax calculation API like **TaxJar** or **Avalara**. These services can calculate taxes based on real-time location, current tax rates, and special rules (e.g., sales tax holidays, exemptions).

- **Example Integration with TaxJar** (a third-party API for tax calculation):

```php
php

$url = 'https://api.taxjar.com/v2/taxes';
```

```php
$api_key = 'your_taxjar_api_key';

// Prepare data for the API request
$data = [
    'to_country' => 'US',
    'to_zip'                        =>
$_SESSION['user_zip_code'],
    'amount' => $total_product_cost,
    'shipping' => $shipping_cost
];

$headers = [
    'Authorization: Bearer ' . $api_key,
    'Content-Type: application/json'
];

$ch = curl_init($url);
curl_setopt($ch,    CURLOPT_RETURNTRANSFER,
true);
curl_setopt($ch, CURLOPT_POST, true);
curl_setopt($ch,        CURLOPT_POSTFIELDS,
json_encode($data));
curl_setopt($ch,        CURLOPT_HTTPHEADER,
$headers);

$response = curl_exec($ch);
$response_data  =  json_decode($response,
true);
```

```php
// Get tax amount from the API response
$tax_amount                        =
$response_data['tax']['amount_to_collect'
];

// Add tax to the total order cost
$total_order_cost = $total_product_cost +
$shipping_cost + $tax_amount;
```

- **Considerations**: Using a tax API ensures that taxes are calculated accurately according to the latest rules and rates. This is especially useful for businesses operating in multiple regions with different tax rules.

Integrating with Shipping Providers (FedEx, UPS, etc.)

For more advanced shipping options, such as real-time shipping rates and labels, you can integrate with third-party shipping providers like **FedEx**, **UPS**, or **USPS**. These services provide APIs that allow you to calculate shipping costs, print shipping labels, and track shipments.

1. Integrating FedEx or UPS for Shipping Rates

To integrate with a shipping provider like FedEx or UPS, you'll need to sign up for their developer API and obtain an API key. The APIs provide endpoints for calculating shipping rates, tracking shipments, and generating shipping labels.

- **FedEx Shipping API**: You can integrate FedEx's API to get real-time shipping rates based on the user's shipping address and package details.

Example of Using the FedEx API (simplified):

```php
php

// FedEx API endpoint and authentication
details
$url  =  'https://gateway.fedex.com/web-
services';
$api_key = 'your_fedex_api_key';

// Create a request to get shipping rates
$data = [
    'from_address'                    =>
$_SESSION['user_address'],
    'to_address' => $shipping_address,
    'weight' => $total_weight,
    'dimensions' => $product_dimensions
];

// Send request to FedEx API and get the
shipping rates
$response = send_api_request($url, $data);
$shipping_rates                           =
$response['shipping_rates'];
```

203

```
// Calculate the total shipping cost
$shipping_cost                          =
$shipping_rates['standard'];

// Add the shipping cost to the total order
cost
$total_order_cost = $total_product_cost +
$shipping_cost;
```

- o **Send API Request**: The send_api_request() function would handle sending the request to FedEx's API and receiving the response.
- o **Rate Calculation**: FedEx or UPS will return various shipping options with different costs and delivery times.

2. Printing Shipping Labels:

Once an order is placed, you can use the shipping provider's API to print a shipping label. The API will provide a downloadable link to the shipping label, which you can then print and attach to the package.

Example of Generating a Shipping Label with FedEx:

php

```
$label_url                              =
generate_shipping_label($shipping_data);
// Provide the user with a link to download the
shipping label
echo "<a href='$label_url' download>Download
Shipping Label</a>";
```

- **Considerations**: Shipping API integrations allow you to offer real-time shipping rates to your customers, which can improve the accuracy of shipping costs. It also automates the process of generating shipping labels and tracking shipments, saving time and reducing errors.

Conclusion

By the end of this chapter, you should have a comprehensive understanding of how to implement **shipping and tax calculation** for your e-commerce site. You've learned how to:

1. **Offer multiple shipping options**, such as flat rate, weight-based, and price-based shipping.
2. **Calculate taxes** based on the user's location, either manually or by using a tax API.
3. **Integrate with shipping providers** like FedEx and UPS for real-time shipping rates, tracking, and label generation.

Implementing these features will enhance the customer experience by offering transparent and accurate shipping and tax information, while also streamlining your business operations by integrating with shipping providers and automating key processes.

CHAPTER 18

EMAIL NOTIFICATIONS AND USER COMMUNICATION

Effective communication with customers is crucial in e-commerce. Email notifications serve as a vital tool to keep customers informed about their orders, shipments, and promotional offers. In this chapter, we will cover how to send **order confirmations**, **shipping updates**, and **newsletters** using **PHPMailer**, along with how to implement **email templates** for different scenarios to create a seamless communication process.

Sending Order Confirmations, Shipping Updates, and Newsletters

1. **Order Confirmation Emails**: Order confirmation emails are essential for providing customers with a summary of their purchase and letting them know that their order is being processed. These emails should include details such as the order number, items purchased, and estimated delivery date.

2. **Shipping Update Emails**: Shipping update emails keep customers informed about the status of their order, including when it has been shipped, any tracking information, and expected delivery times.

3. **Newsletters**: Sending newsletters is a great way to engage with your customers by promoting new products, seasonal sales, or offering exclusive discounts. Newsletters should be visually appealing and personalized to keep your customers interested.

Using PHPMailer for Sending Emails

PHPMailer is a popular PHP library for sending emails. It provides a simple and flexible way to send emails through various protocols (SMTP, mail(), or sendmail). PHPMailer is ideal for sending both plain-text and HTML emails, supporting attachments, and ensuring email delivery.

1. Installing PHPMailer:

First, install PHPMailer via **Composer** if you haven't already:

```bash
```

```
composer require phpmailer/phpmailer
```

Alternatively, you can download PHPMailer manually from its GitHub repository.

2. Sending an Email with PHPMailer:

Here's how you can send an email using PHPMailer. We'll create a basic order confirmation email, but this can be extended to any type of notification (e.g., shipping updates, newsletters).

File: /email/order-confirmation.php:

php

```php
<?php
use PHPMailer\PHPMailer\PHPMailer;
use PHPMailer\PHPMailer\Exception;

require 'vendor/autoload.php';   // Include the
PHPMailer autoloader

// Create an instance of PHPMailer
$mail = new PHPMailer(true);

try {
    // Server settings
    $mail->isSMTP();
// Set mailer to use SMTP
    $mail->Host      =      'smtp.yourdomain.com';
// Specify main SMTP server
    $mail->SMTPAuth           =            true;
// Enable SMTP authentication
```

```php
    $mail->Username                       =
'your_email@yourdomain.com';            //
SMTP username
    $mail->Password   =   'your_email_password';
// SMTP password
    $mail->SMTPSecure                     =
PHPMailer::ENCRYPTION_STARTTLS;          //
Enable TLS encryption
    $mail->Port               =           587;
// TCP port for SMTP

    // Recipients
    $mail->setFrom('no-reply@yourstore.com',
'Your Store');        // Sender's email
    $mail->addAddress($user_email,  $user_name);
// Recipient's email (user's email)

    // Content
    $mail->isHTML(true);
// Set email format to HTML
    $mail->Subject = 'Order Confirmation - Your
Order #12345';      // Subject
    $mail->Body   = 'Thank you for your purchase!
Your  order   <strong>#12345</strong>  has  been
confirmed. You will receive a shipping update
soon.';  // Email content (HTML)

    // Send the email
    $mail->send();
```

```php
    echo 'Order confirmation email has been
sent.';
} catch (Exception $e) {
    echo "Message could not be sent. Mailer
Error: {$mail->ErrorInfo}";
}
?>
```

- **Server Settings**: Configure the SMTP settings with your email provider's details (e.g., Gmail, SendGrid, Mailgun, etc.).
- **Recipients**: Set the recipient's email address and the sender's address.
- **Content**: Write the subject and body of the email. You can use HTML to format the email content and make it visually appealing.

3. Sending Shipping Update Emails:

You can adapt the order confirmation email to send shipping updates by modifying the subject and content of the email.

File: /email/shipping-update.php:

php

```php
<?php
use PHPMailer\PHPMailer\PHPMailer;
use PHPMailer\PHPMailer\Exception;
```

```php
require 'vendor/autoload.php';   // Include the
PHPMailer autoloader

// Create an instance of PHPMailer
$mail = new PHPMailer(true);

try {
    // Server settings
    $mail->isSMTP();
// Set mailer to use SMTP
    $mail->Host      =     'smtp.yourdomain.com';
// Specify main SMTP server
    $mail->SMTPAuth          =          true;
// Enable SMTP authentication
    $mail->Username                          =
'your_email@yourdomain.com';                  //
SMTP username
    $mail->Password   =    'your_email_password';
// SMTP password
    $mail->SMTPSecure                        =
PHPMailer::ENCRYPTION_STARTTLS;               //
Enable TLS encryption
    $mail->Port              =             587;
// TCP port for SMTP

    // Recipients
    $mail->setFrom('no-reply@yourstore.com',
'Your Store');       // Sender's email
```

```php
$mail->addAddress($user_email, $user_name);
// Recipient's email (user's email)

    // Content
    $mail->isHTML(true);
// Set email format to HTML
    $mail->Subject = 'Your Order #12345 has
Shipped';              // Subject
    $mail->Body              = 'Your    order
<strong>#12345</strong> has been shipped! You can
track your order using the following tracking
number: <strong>1234567890</strong>. Thank you
for shopping with us!';  // Email content (HTML)

    // Send the email
    $mail->send();
    echo 'Shipping update email has been sent.';
} catch (Exception $e) {
    echo "Message could not be sent. Mailer
Error: {$mail->ErrorInfo}";
}
?>
```

- Modify the email content to include tracking numbers or estimated delivery dates to keep customers updated about their orders.

Implementing Email Templates for Different Scenarios

Email templates allow you to create reusable email structures for various events, such as order confirmations, shipping updates, newsletters, and more. By using email templates, you can maintain consistency in your messaging and branding.

1. Creating Email Templates:

You can create HTML-based templates for your emails. Here's an example of an email template for an order confirmation.

File: /email/templates/order-confirmation-template.php:

php

```
<!DOCTYPE html>
<html lang="en">
<head>
    <meta charset="UTF-8">
    <meta name="viewport" content="width=device-width, initial-scale=1.0">
    <title>Order Confirmation</title>
    <style>
        body { font-family: Arial, sans-serif;
margin: 0; padding: 0; background-color: #f4f4f4;
}
```

```
        .container {  width:  80%;  margin:  20px
auto;  padding:  20px;  background-color:  #fff;
border-radius: 8px; }
        .header {  text-align:  center;  padding:
20px; background-color: #007bff; color: #fff; }
        .footer {  text-align:  center;  padding:
10px;  background-color:  #f1f1f1;  color:  #333;
font-size: 12px; }
    </style>
</head>
<body>
    <div class="container">
        <div class="header">
            <h1>Thank    you    for    your    order,
{USER_NAME}!</h1>
        </div>
        <h2>Order Details:</h2>
        <p><strong>Order           ID:</strong>
{ORDER_ID}</p>
        <p><strong>Order           Date:</strong>
{ORDER_DATE}</p>
        <p><strong>Total          Amount:</strong>
{TOTAL_AMOUNT}</p>

        <h3>Items in your order:</h3>
        <ul>
            <li>Item 1 - {ITEM_1}</li>
            <li>Item 2 - {ITEM_2}</li>
            <li>Item 3 - {ITEM_3}</li>
```

```
        </ul>

        <p>You will receive an email once your
order has been shipped.</p>
        <div class="footer">
            <p>&; 2025 YourStore. All Rights
Reserved.</p>
        </div>
    </div>
</body>
</html>
```

In the template above, placeholders like {USER_NAME}, {ORDER_ID}, and {ITEM_1} will be replaced dynamically with actual data when sending the email.

2. Sending Emails Using Templates:

You can load and replace placeholders in the template with actual values when sending an email.

File: /email/send-email-with-template.php:

php

```php
<?php
use PHPMailer\PHPMailer\PHPMailer;
use PHPMailer\PHPMailer\Exception;
```

```php
require 'vendor/autoload.php';   // Include the
PHPMailer autoloader

// Create an instance of PHPMailer
$mail = new PHPMailer(true);

try {
    // Load the email template
    $template                               =
file_get_contents('templates/order-
confirmation-template.php');

    // Replace placeholders with actual data
    $template    =    str_replace('{USER_NAME}',
$user_name, $template);
    $template    =    str_replace('{ORDER_ID}',
$order_id, $template);
    $template    =    str_replace('{ORDER_DATE}',
$order_date, $template);
    $template   =   str_replace('{TOTAL_AMOUNT}',
$total_amount, $template);
    $template = str_replace('{ITEM_1}', $item_1,
$template);
    $template = str_replace('{ITEM_2}', $item_2,
$template);
    $template = str_replace('{ITEM_3}', $item_3,
$template);

    // Server settings
```

217

```php
    $mail->isSMTP();
// Set mailer to use SMTP
    $mail->Host       =       'smtp.yourdomain.com';
// Specify main SMTP server
    $mail->SMTPAuth             =             true;
// Enable SMTP authentication
    $mail->Username                             =
'your_email@yourdomain.com';                     //
SMTP username
    $mail->Password   =   'your_email_password';
// SMTP password
    $mail->SMTPSecure                           =
PHPMailer::ENCRYPTION_STARTTLS;                  //
Enable TLS encryption
    $mail->Port               =               587;
// TCP port for SMTP

    // Recipients
    $mail->setFrom('no-reply@yourstore.com',
'Your Store');          // Sender's email
    $mail->addAddress($user_email,  $user_name);
// Recipient's email (user's email)

    // Content
    $mail->isHTML(true);
// Set email format to HTML
    $mail->Subject = 'Order Confirmation - Your
Order #' . $order_id;  // Subject
```

```
$mail->Body    = $template;  // Email content
(HTML from template)

    // Send the email
    $mail->send();
    echo 'Order confirmation email has been
sent.';
} catch (Exception $e) {
    echo "Message could not be sent. Mailer
Error: {$mail->ErrorInfo}";
}
?>
```

- **Loading the Template**: The email template is loaded using `file_get_contents()`.
- **Replacing Placeholders**: We replace the placeholders in the template (e.g., {USER_NAME}) with actual data (e.g., $user_name).
- **Sending the Email**: The email is sent using PHPMailer with the dynamically generated content from the template.

Conclusion

By the end of this chapter, you should have a fully functional email system in place to handle important notifications for your e-commerce store. You've learned how to:

1. Send **order confirmation emails, shipping updates**, and **newsletters** using **PHPMailer**.

2. Implement **email templates** to create consistent and reusable email structures.

3. Dynamically populate email content using templates to personalize communication with your customers.

Effective email communication helps build trust, keep customers informed, and promote your products, leading to better customer retention and increased sales.

CHAPTER 19

CREATING AN ADMIN DASHBOARD

An **Admin Dashboard** is a crucial tool for managing the backend of an e-commerce store. It allows administrators to efficiently manage products, orders, users, and view sales reports. In this chapter, we will walk through the steps to build a **secure admin interface**, implement **filtering and sorting functionality**, and manage **inventory** and **sales reports**.

Building a Secure Admin Interface to Manage Products, Orders, and Users

A secure admin interface is essential for ensuring that only authorized users (administrators) can access sensitive management features such as product management, order tracking, and user management.

1. Securing the Admin Area:

The first step in building a secure admin dashboard is to authenticate and authorize users. Use session management to ensure only authorized users can access the admin panel.

- **Create a login system for admin users**:

```php
php

// admin_login.php
session_start();

// Check if the form is submitted
if (isset($_POST['login'])) {
    $username = $_POST['username'];
    $password = $_POST['password'];

    // Authenticate the admin user
    include 'db.php';
    $sql = "SELECT * FROM users WHERE
username = ? AND role = 'admin'";
    $stmt = $conn->prepare($sql);
    $stmt->bind_param("s", $username);
    $stmt->execute();
    $result = $stmt->get_result();
    $user = $result->fetch_assoc();

    // Verify the password
    if              ($user              &&
password_verify($password,
$user['password'])) {
        $_SESSION['admin_logged_in']    =
true;
        $_SESSION['admin_id']           =
$user['user_id'];
```

```
        header("Location: dashboard.php");
    } else {
        echo "Invalid login credentials.";
    }
}
```

- o The above code verifies that the admin user is valid based on the username and password.
- o The role = 'admin' ensures that only admin users can log in.

- **Access control:**

Protect all admin pages by checking if the user is logged in as an admin.

php

```
// admin_access.php
session_start();

if    (!isset($_SESSION['admin_logged_in'])
||  $_SESSION['admin_logged_in']  !==  true)
{
    header("Location: admin_login.php");
    exit();
}
```

- o If the session variable admin_logged_in is not set, the user is redirected to the login page.

2. Admin Dashboard Interface:

The admin dashboard should be intuitive, showing key features such as managing products, orders, and users, as well as quick access to reports.

- **HTML and PHP for the Dashboard Layout**:

    File: /admin/dashboard.php:

    php

```php
<?php
session_start();

if   (!isset($_SESSION['admin_logged_in'])
|| $_SESSION['admin_logged_in'] !== true)
{
    header("Location: admin_login.php");
    exit();
}
?>

<html lang="en">
<head>
    <meta charset="UTF-8">
    <meta                 name="viewport"
content="width=device-width,      initial-
scale=1.0">
```

```
<title>Admin Dashboard</title>
<link              rel="stylesheet"
href="styles.css">
</head>
<body>
    <header>
        <h1>Welcome          to          Admin
Dashboard</h1>
        <a href="logout.php">Logout</a>
    </header>

    <nav>
        <ul>
            <li><a             href="manage-
products.php">Manage Products</a></li>
            <li><a             href="manage-
orders.php">Manage Orders</a></li>
            <li><a             href="manage-
users.php">Manage Users</a></li>
            <li><a              href="sales-
reports.php">Sales Reports</a></li>
        </ul>
    </nav>
</body>
</html>
```

o   The dashboard consists of navigation links to
    various sections such as product management,
    order management, and user management.

o **Logout** functionality allows admins to log out securely.

Adding Filtering and Sorting Functionality for Better Admin Control

To enhance the admin's control over products, orders, and users, we can add filtering and sorting functionality. This helps administrators easily search for specific items or orders and manage them effectively.

1. Filtering Products:

In the **Manage Products** section, an admin might want to filter products by category, price range, or availability.

- **Filter Products by Category**:

php

```php
// File: /admin/manage-products.php
session_start();
include 'db.php';

$category_filter                    =
isset($_GET['category'])            ?
$_GET['category'] : '';

$sql = "SELECT * FROM products WHERE
category_id LIKE ?";
```

```php
$stmt = $conn->prepare($sql);
$stmt->bind_param("s", $category_filter);
$stmt->execute();
$result = $stmt->get_result();

// Display products in table format
echo "<table>";
echo "<tr><th>Product Name</th><th>Price</th><th>Category</th><th>Actions</th></tr>";
while ($product = $result->fetch_assoc())
{
    echo "<tr>";
    echo "<td>" . $product['name'] . "</td>";
    echo "<td>" . $product['price'] . "</td>";
    echo "<td>" . $product['category_id'] . "</td>";
    echo "<td><a href='edit-product.php?id=" . $product['product_id'] . "'>Edit</a> | <a href='delete-product.php?id=" . $product['product_id'] . "'>Delete</a></td>";
    echo "</tr>";
}
echo "</table>";
```

o **SQL Query**: The products are filtered based on the selected category, which is passed as a GET parameter.

o **Displaying Results**: The filtered products are displayed in a table with actions like "Edit" and "Delete."

2. Sorting Products:

Allow admins to sort products by price, name, or date added.

- **Sort Products by Price**:

php

```
$sort_by = isset($_GET['sort_by']) ?
$_GET['sort_by'] : 'name'; // Default sort
by name
$sql = "SELECT * FROM products ORDER BY
$sort_by";
```

o The admin can choose whether to sort products by name, price, or date.

Managing Inventory and Sales Reports

1. Managing Inventory:

The admin should be able to manage the inventory by updating the stock quantities of products.

- **Inventory Update**:

php

```
// File: /admin/manage-inventory.php
session_start();
include 'db.php';

if (isset($_POST['update_stock'])) {
    $product_id = $_POST['product_id'];
    $new_stock = $_POST['new_stock'];

    $sql    =    "UPDATE    products    SET
stock_quantity = ? WHERE product_id = ?";
    $stmt = $conn->prepare($sql);
    $stmt->bind_param("ii",    $new_stock,
$product_id);
    $stmt->execute();
    echo        "Inventory        updated
successfully!";
}
```

- o **Updating Stock**: Admins can adjust stock
  quantities directly from the inventory page,
  ensuring that the inventory data is up-to-date.

2. Generating Sales Reports:

Sales reports allow admins to analyze revenue, track product sales, and monitor business performance. This is essential for making informed decisions.

- **Generating a Simple Sales Report**:

```php
// File: /admin/sales-reports.php
session_start();
include 'db.php';

// Get sales data
$sql = "SELECT p.name, SUM(od.quantity) AS
total_sales, SUM(od.quantity * p.price) AS
total_revenue
        FROM order_details od
        JOIN products p ON od.product_id =
p.product_id
        GROUP BY p.name
        ORDER BY total_sales DESC";
$result = $conn->query($sql);

echo "<h3>Sales Report</h3>";
echo "<table>";
echo        "<tr><th>Product</th><th>Total
Sales</th><th>Total Revenue</th></tr>";
```

```php
while ($report = $result->fetch_assoc()) {
    echo "<tr>";
    echo  "<td>"  .  $report['name']  .
"</td>";
    echo "<td>" . $report['total_sales'] .
"</td>";
    echo "<td>" . $report['total_revenue']
. "</td>";
    echo "</tr>";
}
echo "</table>";
```

- o **SQL Query**: This query calculates the total sales (quantity sold) and total revenue for each product, grouping the results by product name.
- o **Displaying Results**: The sales report shows the total sales and revenue for each product.

Conclusion

By the end of this chapter, you should have a fully functional and secure **admin dashboard** for managing your e-commerce store. You have learned how to:

1. **Secure the admin area** using login systems and session management.
2. **Add filtering and sorting functionality** for managing products and orders.

231

3. **Implement inventory management** to update stock quantities.

4. **Generate and display sales reports** to analyze business performance.

This admin dashboard will give you complete control over your e-commerce store, improving operational efficiency and enabling you to make data-driven decisions.

CHAPTER 20

PERFORMANCE OPTIMIZATION

Performance is crucial in e-commerce. A slow-loading website can lead to poor user experience, lower conversion rates, and ultimately, lost sales. Optimizing your e-commerce site for speed and efficiency will help enhance the customer experience, improve your SEO rankings, and reduce server load. In this chapter, we'll cover **caching strategies, optimizing database queries**, and **using Content Delivery Networks (CDNs)** to serve static assets efficiently.

Caching Strategies to Improve Site Speed

Caching is a technique used to temporarily store data in memory so that future requests for the same data can be served faster, without requiring the system to fetch or compute the data again. Proper use of caching can significantly speed up your website by reducing load times and server processing.

1. Browser Caching:

Browser caching allows static resources (such as images, CSS, and JavaScript files) to be stored in the user's browser. This way, users do not need to re-download these resources every time they visit the site, improving performance on subsequent visits.

- **How to Implement**: Use the .htaccess file (for Apache servers) to set expiration headers for static files. These headers tell the browser how long to store resources before checking for updates.

Example of enabling browser caching in .htaccess:

apache

```
<IfModule mod_expires.c>
    ExpiresActive On
    ExpiresDefault "access plus 1 month"
    ExpiresByType image/jpg "access plus 1 month"
    ExpiresByType image/jpeg "access plus 1 month"
    ExpiresByType image/png "access plus 1 month"
    ExpiresByType text/css "access plus 1 month"
    ExpiresByType application/javascript "access plus 1 month"
    ExpiresByType text/javascript "access plus 1 month"
</IfModule>
```

  o This will store the images, CSS, and JavaScript files in the user's browser for 1 month.

234

2. Server-Side Caching:

Server-side caching can be done by caching dynamic content, such as HTML pages or database queries, in memory. This avoids the need to regenerate the content or query the database every time a user visits the site.

- **Types of Server-Side Caching**:
  - **Opcode Cache (e.g., OPcache)**: Caches compiled PHP code in memory to speed up script execution. Enable OPcache to cache the compiled bytecode of your PHP scripts.

    Example of enabling OPcache in `php.ini`:

    ```ini
    ini
    ```

    ```ini
    opcache.enable=1
    opcache.memory_consumption=128
    ```

  - **Data Caching (e.g., Redis, Memcached)**: Cache frequently accessed data such as user sessions or product information using an in-memory store like **Redis** or **Memcached**. This allows you to serve data faster without querying the database.

    Example of using Redis for caching:

    ```php
    php
    ```

235

```
$redis = new Redis();
$redis->connect('127.0.0.1', 6379);

// Set cache with a 1-hour expiration
time
$redis->setex('product_123',   3600,
json_encode($product_data));
```

- **Database Query Caching**: Cache results
  of frequently executed database queries.
  This is particularly helpful for queries
  that return data that does not change
  often, such as product listings or user
  profiles.

3. Page Caching:

Page caching stores the entire HTML output of a page, so it
doesn't have to be regenerated every time a user visits it. This is
particularly useful for static pages or product pages that don't
change frequently.

- **Implementing Page Caching**: You can use tools like
  Varnish Cache or **Nginx** to cache entire pages. For PHP-
  based sites, using **full-page caching** can reduce the load
  on the web server by serving static HTML instead of
  dynamically generated content.

236

Example of using a caching plugin in WordPress:

- o Install and configure caching plugins such as **WP Super Cache** or **W3 Total Cache** to enable page caching.

Optimizing Database Queries and Reducing Server Load

A slow database can significantly affect the performance of your e-commerce site, especially when dealing with large amounts of data or complex queries.

1. Optimize Queries:

Efficient database queries are key to improving performance. Avoid using SELECT * queries, and instead, query only the necessary fields. Additionally, use indexes to speed up searches and joins.

- **Example of optimizing a query**:

sql

```
-- Inefficient query
SELECT * FROM products WHERE category_id =
3;

-- Optimized query
```

237

```
SELECT  product_id,  name,  price  FROM
products WHERE category_id = 3;
```

- **Indexes**: Add indexes on frequently queried columns, such as product IDs or category IDs, to speed up search queries.

Example of adding an index:

```
sql
```

```
CREATE  INDEX  idx_category_id  ON  products
(category_id);
```

2. Use Query Caching:

Most modern databases, like MySQL, support query caching. This means that the database will store the result of a query for a certain period, reducing the need to execute the same query multiple times.

- **Enable MySQL Query Cache**: Ensure that your MySQL server has query caching enabled in the `my.cnf` configuration file:

```
ini
```

```
query_cache_type = 1
query_cache_size = 64M
```

3. Database Connection Pooling:

Database connection pooling can reduce the overhead of establishing a new database connection for each request by reusing connections. This is particularly useful in high-traffic sites.

- **Example using PDO (PHP Data Objects)**: You can configure **PDO** to use persistent connections to avoid opening new connections for every request.

```php
$pdo = new PDO("mysql:host=localhost;dbname=yourdb", "username", "password", [
    PDO::ATTR_PERSISTENT => true
]);
```

4. Use Database Replication:

For sites with high traffic, consider using **database replication** to distribute database queries across multiple servers. This can help reduce the load on the primary database and improve read performance.

Using CDNs to Serve Static Assets Efficiently

A **Content Delivery Network (CDN)** is a network of distributed servers that deliver content (images, CSS, JavaScript, etc.) to users based on their geographical location. By serving static assets from a CDN, you can improve load times and reduce server load.

1. Why Use a CDN?

- **Faster Load Times**: By caching content on servers located closer to the user, CDNs reduce latency and increase website speed.
- **Reduced Server Load**: CDNs offload traffic from your main server, preventing it from becoming overloaded during high-traffic events.

2. Integrating a CDN:

To integrate a CDN, you'll need to choose a CDN provider such as **Cloudflare, Amazon CloudFront, KeyCDN,** or **MaxCDN**.

- **How to Use a CDN**:
    - Sign up for a CDN service and follow their setup instructions.
    - Update the URLs of your static assets (images, JavaScript, CSS) to use the CDN domain.

    Example: Instead of:

```
html
```

```
<img
src="https://www.yourstore.com/images/pro
duct1.jpg" alt="Product 1">
```

Use:

```
html
```

```
<img
src="https://cdn.yourstore.com/images/pro
duct1.jpg" alt="Product 1">
```

- **Cache Static Content**:
  - Set appropriate caching headers on the CDN for static content to reduce requests to your origin server.
  - Example of cache-control headers:

    ```
    plaintext
    ```

    ```
    Cache-Control: public, max-age=86400
    // Cache for 24 hours
    ```

3. Dynamic Content Delivery:

Some CDNs, like **Cloudflare**, can cache dynamic content and provide **edge caching** for personalized content, helping speed up the delivery of frequently changing but cacheable data.

Conclusion

By the end of this chapter, you should have a solid understanding of how to optimize your e-commerce site for **performance**. Here's a summary of the techniques covered:

1. **Caching Strategies**:
    o   Implement **browser caching, server-side caching**, and **page caching** to speed up your website.
    o   Use **OPcache, Redis**, or **Memcached** for efficient caching of dynamic content.

2. **Optimizing Database Queries**:
    o   Optimize queries by selecting only necessary fields, adding indexes, and using query caching.
    o   Use **persistent database connections** and **database replication** for high-traffic sites.

3. **Using CDNs**:
    o   Serve static assets via a **CDN** to reduce server load and improve load times.
    o   Cache static content effectively and leverage **edge caching** for dynamic content.

With these optimizations in place, your site will run faster, handle more traffic, and provide a better experience for your users.

CHAPTER 21

IMPLEMENTING MULTI-LANGUAGE AND MULTI-CURRENCY SUPPORT

For an e-commerce website that caters to a global audience, providing multi-language and multi-currency support is essential. This allows customers from different regions to comfortably browse your store in their preferred language and view prices in their local currency. In this chapter, we will walk through the process of implementing **multi-language support**, **multi-currency functionality**, and effectively **managing translations and currency conversion rates**.

Making Your Site Available in Different Languages

When you have customers from different linguistic backgrounds, it's important to make the site accessible in their preferred languages. Multi-language support helps improve user experience and can increase sales by breaking down language barriers.

1. Setting Up Multi-Language Support

To implement multi-language support, you will need a way to store and manage translations for your content (e.g., product names, descriptions, and buttons). There are two main approaches to multi-language implementation:

- **Static Translation Files**: You can store translations in separate files (e.g., JSON, XML, or PHP arrays) and load the appropriate file based on the user's selected language.
- **Database Storage**: You can store translations in a database, with each language having its own record for product names, descriptions, etc.

2. Storing Translations in Files (JSON)

Using JSON files for storing translations is a simple and efficient method. Each file will represent a different language and contain the translations for various keys.

- **Example of a translation file** (en.json for English):

json

```
{
    "home": "Home",
    "products": "Products",
    "cart": "Cart",
    "checkout": "Checkout",
```

```json
"add_to_cart": "Add to Cart",
    "welcome_message":    "Welcome    to    our
store!"
}
```

- **Example of a translation file** (fr.json for French):

json

```json
{
    "home": "Accueil",
    "products": "Produits",
    "cart": "Panier",
    "checkout": "Caisse",
    "add_to_cart": "Ajouter au panier",
    "welcome_message":    "Bienvenue    dans
notre magasin !"
}
```

- **Loading Translations Based on the User's Language**:

php

```php
// Load the appropriate language file based
on user selection
$language    =    isset($_GET['lang'])    ?
$_GET['lang']  :  'en';    //  Default  to
English
```

```
$translations                          =
json_decode(file_get_contents("translatio
ns/{$language}.json"), true);


// Display the translation for a specific
key
echo $translations['welcome_message'];
```

3. Dynamic Language Switching:

Provide a language selector so users can switch between available languages.

- **HTML Language Selector**:

```html
html

<select
onchange="window.location.href=this.value
;">
    <option   value="?lang=en"   <?php   if
($language   ==   'en')   echo   'selected';
?>>English</option>
    <option   value="?lang=fr"   <?php   if
($language   ==   'fr')   echo   'selected';
?>>Français</option>
    <!-- Add more languages as needed -->
</select>
```

- **URL Structure**: When a user selects a language, the page reloads with the appropriate language by adding a `lang` parameter to the URL.

4. Database Approach for Translations:

If you want a more dynamic system, store product names, descriptions, and other content in the database. This allows easy updates and management of translations.

- **Example Database Structure**:

sql

```sql
CREATE TABLE products (
    product_id INT AUTO_INCREMENT PRIMARY KEY,
    name_en VARCHAR(255),
    name_fr VARCHAR(255),
    description_en TEXT,
    description_fr TEXT,
    price DECIMAL(10, 2)
);
```

- **Fetching Translated Content**:

php

```php
// Fetch product details based on selected
language
$language   =   isset($_GET['lang'])   ?
$_GET['lang']  :  'en';   // Default to
English
$sql   =   "SELECT   name_{$language},
description_{$language},   price   FROM
products WHERE product_id = ?";
$stmt = $conn->prepare($sql);
$stmt->bind_param("i", $product_id);
$stmt->execute();
$result = $stmt->get_result();
$product = $result->fetch_assoc();
```

Allowing Users to View Prices in Different Currencies

Offering prices in multiple currencies is crucial for providing a better experience to international customers. You can allow users to select their preferred currency, and then convert product prices accordingly.

1. Storing Prices in Base Currency:

It's a good practice to store product prices in a **base currency** (e.g., USD) in the database, and then convert them to the user's preferred currency when displaying them on the website.

- **Example Database Structure**:

```sql
sql
```

```
CREATE TABLE products (
    product_id INT AUTO_INCREMENT PRIMARY
KEY,
    name VARCHAR(255),
    description TEXT,
    price_usd DECIMAL(10, 2)  -- Store the
price in USD
);
```

2. Currency Conversion Logic:

You will need an API or service to fetch real-time exchange rates and convert prices from the base currency to the user's selected currency. Popular options include **Fixer.io**, **Open Exchange Rates**, and **CurrencyLayer**.

- **Example Currency Conversion Using an API**:

php

```php
// Fetch real-time exchange rates from an
API
$currency = isset($_GET['currency']) ?
$_GET['currency'] : 'USD'; // Default to
USD
$api_key = 'your_api_key';
$url = "https://api.exchangerate-
api.com/v4/latest/USD"; // Get exchange
rates for USD
```

```php
$response = file_get_contents($url);
$data = json_decode($response, true);

$exchange_rate                         =
$data['rates'][$currency];    // Get the
conversion rate for the selected currency

// Convert product price to selected
currency
$price_in_selected_currency            =
$product['price_usd'] * $exchange_rate;
```

3. Currency Selector:

Allow users to select their currency, and update the page accordingly.

- **HTML Currency Selector**:

```html
html

<select
onchange="window.location.href=this.value
;">
    <option value="?currency=USD" <?php if
($currency == 'USD') echo 'selected';
?>>USD</option>
```

250

```
    <option value="?currency=EUR" <?php if
($currency == 'EUR') echo 'selected';
?>>EUR</option>
    <option value="?currency=GBP" <?php if
($currency == 'GBP') echo 'selected';
?>>GBP</option>
    <!-- Add more currencies as needed -->
</select>
```

- **Displaying Converted Price**:

```
php
```

```
echo           "<p>Price:        "        .
number_format($price_in_selected_currency
, 2) . " {$currency}</p>";
```

Managing Translations and Currency Conversion Rates

1. **Translation Management**:
   o Maintain a simple system for managing translations through **JSON files**, a **database**, or a **content management system (CMS)**.
   o If you have a large site with frequent content updates, consider using **third-party translation services** like **Google Translate API** or **Microsoft Translator**.

2. **Currency Conversion Rate Management**:

- o Regularly update exchange rates to ensure that the prices are accurate. You can set a schedule to fetch exchange rates from your chosen API and store them in your database.
- o Some **third-party e-commerce platforms** offer built-in multi-currency support, making it easier to manage currencies without custom integration.

Example of a Scheduled Task for Updating Currency Rates:

- **Using Cron Jobs** to automatically update exchange rates every 24 hours:

bash

```
0 0 * * * php /path/to/update-currency-rates.php
```

- **PHP Script to Update Exchange Rates** (update-currency-rates.php):

php

```
$url = "https://api.exchangerate-api.com/v4/latest/USD";
$response = file_get_contents($url);
$data = json_decode($response, true);

$rates = $data['rates'];
```

```
// Store the rates in the database
foreach ($rates as $currency => $rate) {
    $sql = "UPDATE currencies SET rate = ?
WHERE currency_code = ?";
    $stmt = $conn->prepare($sql);
    $stmt->bind_param("ds",          $rate,
$currency);
    $stmt->execute();
}
```

Conclusion

By the end of this chapter, you should have a fully functional **multi-language and multi-currency system** in your e-commerce store. You've learned how to:

1. **Make your site available in multiple languages**, using either static translation files or a database-driven approach.

2. **Allow users to view prices in different currencies**, by converting product prices based on real-time exchange rates.

3. **Manage translations** and **currency conversion rates**, including storing them efficiently and keeping them up-to-date.

Implementing multi-language and multi-currency support will enable you to cater to a global audience, increasing customer satisfaction and broadening your market reach.

CHAPTER 22

HANDLING RETURNS AND CUSTOMER SERVICE

Providing excellent customer service is crucial for the success of any e-commerce business. One of the key aspects of customer service is handling returns efficiently and addressing customer inquiries in a timely and professional manner. In this chapter, we will explore how to build a **returns management system**, offer **customer support**, and create an **FAQ section** to address common issues.

Building a Returns Management System

A returns management system allows customers to initiate returns and exchanges easily. Handling returns efficiently not only improves customer satisfaction but also helps you manage inventory and track return patterns.

1. Creating a Return Policy

First, ensure that your store has a clear and concise return policy. The policy should include information such as:

- **Timeframe for returns** (e.g., 30 days from the purchase date).
- **Condition of items** (e.g., unused, unopened, and in original packaging).
- **Return methods** (e.g., through mail, in-store, or via pickup).
- **Refund or exchange options** (e.g., full refund, store credit, or replacement).
- **Shipping costs** (who pays for the return shipping).

Example of a return policy page:

html

```
<h2>Return Policy</h2>
<p>We want you to be happy with your purchase! If
you're not satisfied with your items, you can
return them within 30 days of the purchase date
for a full refund or exchange.</p>
<ul>
    <li>Items must be unused and in their
original packaging.</li>
    <li>You will be responsible for return
shipping costs unless the item is defective.</li>
    <li>Refunds will be issued to the original
payment method or as store credit.</li>
</ul>
```

<p>If you wish to return an item, please fill out the return form below or contact our support team.</p>

2. Creating a Return Request Form

To allow customers to initiate a return, create a simple return request form that collects relevant information such as order ID, product details, and reason for return.

File: /returns/return-request.php:

php

```
<form method="POST" action="process-return.php">
    <label for="order_id">Order ID:</label>
    <input       type="text"       id="order_id"
name="order_id" required><br>

    <label for="product_id">Product ID:</label>
    <input       type="text"       id="product_id"
name="product_id" required><br>

    <label    for="return_reason">Reason    for
Return:</label>
    <textarea               id="return_reason"
name="return_reason" required></textarea><br>

    <button    type="submit">Submit    Return
Request</button>
```

```
</form>
```

3. Processing the Return Request

When a return request is submitted, the system should validate the request, check that it complies with the return policy, and then initiate the return process (e.g., generating a return label, updating the order status).

File: /returns/process-return.php:

php

```php
<?php
session_start();
include 'db.php';

if ($_SERVER['REQUEST_METHOD'] == 'POST') {
    $order_id = $_POST['order_id'];
    $product_id = $_POST['product_id'];
    $return_reason = $_POST['return_reason'];

    // Check if the order exists and return
policy conditions are met
    $sql = "SELECT * FROM orders WHERE order_id
= ? AND user_id = ?";
    $stmt = $conn->prepare($sql);
    $stmt->bind_param("ii",         $order_id,
$_SESSION['user_id']);
    $stmt->execute();
```

258

```php
$result = $stmt->get_result();
$order = $result->fetch_assoc();

if ($order) {
    // Check if the product is eligible for
return (e.g., within 30 days)
    $date_diff = strtotime('now') -
strtotime($order['order_date']);
    $days = floor($date_diff / (60 * 60 *
24));

    if ($days <= 30) {
        // Process the return: update the
order status and initiate return
        $update_sql = "UPDATE orders SET
return_status = 'Pending' WHERE order_id = ?";
        $stmt = $conn->prepare($update_sql);
        $stmt->bind_param("i", $order_id);
        $stmt->execute();

        // Send confirmation email to the
customer
        mail($order['email'], "Return
Request Received", "Your return request for Order
#$order_id is being processed.");
        echo "Your return request has been
successfully submitted.";
    } else {
```

```
            echo    "Sorry,    returns    are    only
accepted within 30 days of purchase.";
        }
    } else {
        echo "Invalid order ID.";
    }
}
?>
```

- **Order Validation**: The script checks if the order exists and if it is within the allowed return period (e.g., 30 days).
- **Return Status**: The order's return status is updated to 'Pending'.
- **Email Notification**: An email is sent to the customer to inform them that their return request is being processed.

4. Generating Return Labels

Once the return request is approved, you can generate a return shipping label for the customer. Many e-commerce platforms integrate with shipping providers like **FedEx** or **UPS** to create and email return labels.

You can integrate the provider's API to generate return labels automatically. Here's an example of how you can integrate **ShipEngine** to generate return labels.

php

```php
// Example code for generating a return label via
ShipEngine API
$shipEngine                    =                new
ShipEngine\API('your_api_key');
$return_label         =                $shipEngine-
>generateReturnLabel($order_id);

if ($return_label) {
    // Send the return label to the customer
    mail($order['email'], "Your Return Label",
"Click the link to download your return label:
$return_label");
    echo "Return label has been emailed to you.";
}
```

Providing Support for Customers and Managing Inquiries

A robust customer service system is critical for resolving issues promptly and ensuring customer satisfaction.

1. Creating a Support Ticket System

A support ticket system helps track customer issues and inquiries. Customers can submit tickets, which are then assigned to support agents for resolution.

- **Ticket Submission Form**:

  php

```html
<form    method="POST"    action="submit-
ticket.php">
    <label
for="ticket_subject">Subject:</label>
    <input type="text" id="ticket_subject"
name="ticket_subject" required><br>

    <label
for="ticket_message">Message:</label>
    <textarea            id="ticket_message"
name="ticket_message"
required></textarea><br>

    <button            type="submit">Submit
Ticket</button>
</form>
```

- **Processing the Support Ticket**:

File: /support/submit-ticket.php:

php

```php
<?php
session_start();
include 'db.php';

if ($_SERVER['REQUEST_METHOD'] == 'POST')
{
```

```php
    $ticket_subject                        =
$_POST['ticket_subject'];
    $ticket_message                        =
$_POST['ticket_message'];


    // Create a new support ticket in the
database
    $sql = "INSERT INTO support_tickets
(user_id, subject, message) VALUES (?, ?,
?)";
    $stmt = $conn->prepare($sql);
    $stmt->bind_param("iss",
$_SESSION['user_id'],      $ticket_subject,
$ticket_message);
    $stmt->execute();


    // Notify the customer
    echo "Your support ticket has been
submitted. Our team will get back to you
shortly.";
}
?>
```

- **Support Dashboard for Admins**: Create a dashboard for support agents to view and respond to tickets.

2. Handling Inquiries

Ensure timely responses to customer inquiries by organizing and prioritizing support tickets.

- **Support Ticket Status**: Use ticket statuses like 'Open', 'In Progress', and 'Resolved' to manage the workflow.
- **Response Notifications**: Send email notifications to customers when their tickets are updated or resolved.

Creating an FAQ Section and Handling Common Issues

An **FAQ (Frequently Asked Questions)** section can reduce the volume of customer inquiries by providing self-help resources for common issues.

1. Creating the FAQ Section

Create a dedicated page that answers frequently asked questions about shipping, returns, payment methods, and other common concerns.

File: /faq.php:

html

```
<h2>Frequently Asked Questions (FAQ)</h2>

<div class="faq-item">
```

```
<h3>How do I return a product?</h3>
<p>You can return a product within 30 days of
purchase.    Please    visit    our    <a
href="/returns/return-request.php">Return
Page</a> to start the process.</p>
</div>

<div class="faq-item">
    <h3>How can I track my order?</h3>
    <p>You will receive a shipping update with a
tracking number once your order is shipped. You
can   also   track   it   through   your   <a
href="/account/orders.php">Order
History</a>.</p>
</div>

<div class="faq-item">
    <h3>What    are    the    payment    methods
accepted?</h3>
    <p>We accept credit/debit cards, PayPal, and
Apple Pay.</p>
</div>
```

- **Categorizing FAQs**: Group FAQs into categories like "Shipping," "Returns," "Payments," etc., for easier navigation.
- **Searchable FAQ**: Implement a search bar to allow customers to find answers quickly.

2. Handling Common Issues:

Many customer inquiries are related to the same issues, such as tracking orders, processing refunds, or requesting product exchanges. By offering detailed instructions or self-service options in your FAQ section, you can resolve common problems without requiring support tickets.

- **Self-Service Features**: Provide tools like order tracking, return requests, and product exchanges directly through the site, reducing the need for support staff intervention.

Conclusion

By the end of this chapter, you should have a fully functional **returns management system**, an efficient **customer service system**, and an informative **FAQ section**. Here's a summary of what we've covered:

1. **Returns Management System**:
   o Create a process for customers to request returns.
   o Manage and approve returns, generate return labels, and handle refund or exchange options.
2. **Customer Support**:
   o Implement a **support ticket system** to handle customer inquiries and issues.
   o Provide timely responses to customer concerns and keep customers informed.

3. **FAQ Section**:

- o Create an organized FAQ section to answer common customer questions.
- o Use self-service tools to handle issues like order tracking, product returns, and payment inquiries.

With these systems in place, your e-commerce store will be better equipped to handle returns, provide excellent customer support, and address common issues efficiently.

CHAPTER 23

ADVANCED E-COMMERCE FEATURES

As your e-commerce store grows, implementing **advanced features** can greatly enhance the shopping experience, increase conversions, and boost sales. Features like **product recommendations**, **cross-selling**, **wishlists**, **saved carts**, and **discount codes** can help create a more personalized and dynamic experience for your customers. In this chapter, we will explore how to implement these advanced features in your e-commerce site.

Implementing Product Recommendations and Cross-Selling

Product recommendations and cross-selling are powerful tools for increasing the average order value (AOV) and enhancing the customer experience. By suggesting products that complement what the customer is already viewing or has previously purchased, you can guide them toward additional purchases.

1. Product Recommendations:

Product recommendations can be based on several factors, such as:

- **Browsing history**: Suggest products the customer has viewed but hasn't purchased.
- **Similar products**: Suggest products that are similar to the ones the customer is currently viewing.
- **Top-selling products**: Suggest popular products that are highly rated or frequently purchased.

2. Cross-Selling:

Cross-selling is a technique where you recommend products related to what the customer is purchasing. For example, if a customer is buying a laptop, you might recommend a laptop bag, mouse, or keyboard.

Example of Implementing Product Recommendations:

1. **Database Structure**: Store product recommendations and cross-selling relationships in your database. You can create a table that links products based on categories or a similarity score.

sql

```sql
CREATE TABLE product_recommendations (
    product_id INT,
    recommended_product_id INT,
    PRIMARY        KEY        (product_id,
recommended_product_id),
```

```
    FOREIGN KEY (product_id) REFERENCES
products(product_id),
    FOREIGN KEY (recommended_product_id)
REFERENCES products(product_id)
);
```

2. **Fetching Recommendations**: When a user views a product, fetch recommendations based on related products or previous purchases.

php

```php
// Fetch related products based on category
$sql = "SELECT * FROM products WHERE
category_id = ? LIMIT 5";
$stmt = $conn->prepare($sql);
$stmt->bind_param("i", $category_id);
$stmt->execute();
$result = $stmt->get_result();

while ($product = $result->fetch_assoc())
{
    echo "<div class='recommendation'>";
    echo "<img src='" . $product['image']
. "' alt='" . $product['name'] . "'>";
    echo "<p>" . $product['name'] . "</p>";
    echo "</div>";
}
```

o **Related Products**: This code fetches products that belong to the same category as the current product and displays them as recommendations.

3. Cross-Selling Based on Cart Content:

Cross-sell by recommending products related to those already in the user's cart.

php

```php
// Fetch cart items and suggest cross-sells
$cart_items = $_SESSION['cart'];  // Assume cart
items are stored in the session

foreach ($cart_items as $item) {
    $sql = "SELECT * FROM products WHERE
product_id != ? LIMIT 5";
    $stmt = $conn->prepare($sql);
    $stmt->bind_param("i", $item['product_id']);
    $stmt->execute();
    $result = $stmt->get_result();

    while ($product = $result->fetch_assoc()) {
        echo "<div class='cross-sell'>";
        echo "<img src='" . $product['image'] .
"' alt='" . $product['name'] . "'>";
        echo "<p>" . $product['name'] . "</p>";
        echo "</div>";
```

```
        }

}
```

- **Dynamic Cross-Selling**: Based on the items in the cart, you suggest other products that may complement or be related to the customer's current selections.

Creating a Wishlist and Saved Carts for Users

Providing users with the option to save products they are interested in purchasing later (via **wishlists**) or save their cart for future purchases (**saved carts**) can improve engagement and increase the likelihood of future purchases.

1. Creating a Wishlist:

A wishlist allows users to save products for later viewing or purchase. It's a great way to keep potential customers engaged with your store.

- **Database Structure for Wishlist**:

```sql
sql

CREATE TABLE wishlists (
    wishlist_id INT AUTO_INCREMENT PRIMARY
KEY,
    user_id INT,
    product_id INT,
```

```
created_at        TIMESTAMP        DEFAULT
CURRENT_TIMESTAMP,
    FOREIGN   KEY   (user_id)   REFERENCES
users(user_id),
    FOREIGN   KEY   (product_id)   REFERENCES
products(product_id)
);
```

- **Adding Items to Wishlist**:

php

```php
// Add item to wishlist
$sql = "INSERT INTO wishlists (user_id,
product_id) VALUES (?, ?)";
$stmt = $conn->prepare($sql);
$stmt->bind_param("ii",
$_SESSION['user_id'], $product_id);
$stmt->execute();
echo "Product added to your wishlist.";
```

- **Displaying Wishlist Items**:

php

```php
// Fetch wishlist items
$sql = "SELECT * FROM wishlists WHERE
user_id = ?";
$stmt = $conn->prepare($sql);
```

```
$stmt->bind_param("i",
$_SESSION['user_id']);
$stmt->execute();
$result = $stmt->get_result();

while ($item = $result->fetch_assoc()) {
    echo "<div class='wishlist-item'>";
    echo "<p>" . $item['name'] . "</p>";
    echo        "<a        href='remove-from-
wishlist.php?id=" . $item['product_id'] .
"'>Remove</a>";
    echo "</div>";
}
```

o Users can view their saved items and remove products if they are no longer interested.

2. Creating Saved Carts:

Saved carts allow users to store their shopping cart contents for future purchases. This is particularly useful for customers who want to buy products but need more time to complete the purchase.

- **Database Structure for Saved Carts**:

```sql
CREATE TABLE saved_carts (
```

```
    cart_id  INT  AUTO_INCREMENT  PRIMARY
KEY,
    user_id INT,
    product_id INT,
    quantity INT,
    created_at       TIMESTAMP       DEFAULT
CURRENT_TIMESTAMP,
    FOREIGN  KEY  (user_id)  REFERENCES
users(user_id),
    FOREIGN  KEY  (product_id)  REFERENCES
products(product_id)
);
```

- **Saving a Cart**:

php

```php
// Save cart for later
foreach ($_SESSION['cart'] as $item) {
    $sql  =  "INSERT  INTO  saved_carts
(user_id, product_id, quantity) VALUES (?,
?, ?)";
    $stmt = $conn->prepare($sql);
    $stmt->bind_param("iii",
$_SESSION['user_id'], $item['product_id'],
$item['quantity']);
    $stmt->execute();
}
echo "Your cart has been saved for later.";
```

- **Retrieving a Saved Cart**:

php

```php
// Retrieve saved cart
$sql = "SELECT * FROM saved_carts WHERE
user_id = ?";
$stmt = $conn->prepare($sql);
$stmt->bind_param("i",
$_SESSION['user_id']);
$stmt->execute();
$result = $stmt->get_result();

while ($cart_item = $result->fetch_assoc()) {
    echo "<div class='cart-item'>";
    echo "<p>" . $cart_item['name'] . " x
" . $cart_item['quantity'] . "</p>";
    echo "<a href='add-to-cart.php?id=" .
$cart_item['product_id'] . "'>Add to
Cart</a>";
    echo "</div>";
}
```

Offering Discount Codes and Promotional Campaigns

Discount codes and promotional campaigns are essential tools for attracting customers, increasing sales, and rewarding loyal customers.

1. Creating Discount Codes:

Discount codes allow you to provide special offers, such as percentage-based discounts or fixed amount off a total purchase.

- **Database Structure for Discount Codes**:

sql

```sql
CREATE TABLE discount_codes (
    code_id   INT   AUTO_INCREMENT   PRIMARY KEY,
    code VARCHAR(50) UNIQUE,
    discount_type         ENUM('percentage',
'fixed') NOT NULL,
    discount_value   DECIMAL(10,   2)   NOT
NULL,
    expiration_date DATE,
    is_active BOOLEAN DEFAULT TRUE
);
```

- **Adding a Discount Code**:

php

```php
$code = $_POST['discount_code'];
$sql = "SELECT * FROM discount_codes WHERE
code  =  ?  AND  is_active  =  TRUE  AND
expiration_date >= CURDATE()";
$stmt = $conn->prepare($sql);
```

```php
$stmt->bind_param("s", $code);
$stmt->execute();
$result = $stmt->get_result();
$discount = $result->fetch_assoc();

if ($discount) {
    if    ($discount['discount_type']    ==
'percentage') {
        $discount_amount                 =
($total_order_cost                        *
$discount['discount_value']) / 100;
    } else {
        $discount_amount                 =
$discount['discount_value'];
    }

    $total_order_cost -= $discount_amount;
    echo "Discount applied! Total amount
after          discount:          $"        .
number_format($total_order_cost, 2);
} else {
    echo "Invalid or expired discount
code.";
}
```

2. Managing Promotional Campaigns:

Promotional campaigns can include discounts, flash sales, or bundle deals. You can manage these campaigns by creating special time-limited promotions that apply automatically to the cart.

- **Example of Flash Sale**:

```php
php

$flash_sale_start = '2025-12-01';
$flash_sale_end = '2025-12-31';
$current_date = date('Y-m-d');

if ($current_date >= $flash_sale_start &&
$current_date <= $flash_sale_end) {
    $discount_percentage = 20;   // 20% off
during flash sale
    $total_order_cost                   -=
($total_order_cost * $discount_percentage)
/ 100;
    echo   "Flash   sale   active!   You've
received a 20% discount.";
}
```

Conclusion

By the end of this chapter, you should have implemented several **advanced e-commerce features** that will enhance user experience and improve sales:

1. **Product Recommendations and Cross-Selling**: Encourage additional purchases by suggesting related products.

2. **Wishlists and Saved Carts**: Allow customers to save their favorite products or carts for later purchase.

3. **Discount Codes and Promotional Campaigns**: Attract customers with special offers, discounts, and time-sensitive promotions.

These advanced features help increase customer engagement, provide a personalized shopping experience, and incentivize repeat purchases, ultimately driving sales and improving business performance.

CHAPTER 24

SCALING YOUR E-COMMERCE WEBSITE

As your e-commerce store grows, it's essential to ensure that it can handle increasing traffic, process more orders, and manage large volumes of data efficiently. Scaling your website involves not only improving performance and reliability but also ensuring that the infrastructure is flexible enough to accommodate future growth. In this chapter, we will explore strategies for **scaling your website**, including handling high traffic with **load balancers**, scaling **horizontally** using **cloud services**, and **optimizing database performance** for large datasets.

Handling High Traffic and Scaling with Load Balancers

When your e-commerce site experiences high traffic, it's essential to distribute the load across multiple servers to ensure that no single server becomes overwhelmed. **Load balancing** is a technique used to distribute incoming traffic across multiple servers, improving the site's availability, reliability, and performance.

1. What is Load Balancing?

Load balancing involves using a **load balancer** to distribute traffic among multiple web servers. This helps avoid server overload and ensures that users can access the site even if one or more servers fail.

There are several types of load balancing algorithms:

- **Round Robin**: Distributes traffic evenly across all available servers.
- **Least Connections**: Directs traffic to the server with the least active connections.
- **IP Hash**: Routes traffic based on the IP address of the client.

2. Implementing Load Balancing

To implement load balancing, you can use software or hardware-based load balancers. Popular software load balancers include **Nginx, HAProxy**, and **AWS Elastic Load Balancer (ELB)**.

Example of configuring Nginx as a Load Balancer:

1. **Install Nginx** on a dedicated server that will act as the load balancer.
2. **Configure Nginx for load balancing** by editing the configuration file (/etc/nginx/nginx.conf):

```
nginx

http {
    upstream backend_servers {
        server webserver1.example.com;
        server webserver2.example.com;
        server webserver3.example.com;
    }

    server {
        listen 80;

        location / {
            proxy_pass
http://backend_servers;
            proxy_set_header Host $host;
            proxy_set_header    X-Real-IP
$remote_addr;
            proxy_set_header  X-Forwarded-
For $proxy_add_x_forwarded_for;
        }
    }
}
```

3. **Explanation**:

   o **upstream backend_servers**: Defines a
   group of backend servers where traffic will be
   distributed.

- o **`proxy_pass`**: Forwards the incoming requests to the backend servers.
- o **`proxy_set_header`**: Passes the original headers from the client to the backend servers.

3. Auto-Scaling with Cloud Providers

Most cloud providers offer **auto-scaling** features that automatically add or remove servers based on traffic demands. For instance, **AWS EC2**, **Google Cloud Compute Engine**, and **Azure Virtual Machines** provide scalable infrastructure that automatically adjusts to traffic loads.

Example: AWS Auto Scaling:

- AWS can automatically launch additional EC2 instances when traffic spikes and terminate them when the load decreases.
- **Elastic Load Balancing (ELB)** automatically distributes traffic across all available EC2 instances.

Using Cloud Services to Scale Horizontally

Scaling horizontally involves adding more servers to your infrastructure to handle increased traffic and load. Cloud services make horizontal scaling easy by allowing you to spin up new instances or containers on-demand.

1. Why Scale Horizontally?

Horizontal scaling is more cost-effective and flexible than vertical scaling (adding more power to a single server) because it allows you to distribute the load across multiple servers. As your e-commerce store grows, you can keep adding servers to handle traffic surges, such as during sales events or holiday seasons.

2. Using Cloud Providers for Horizontal Scaling

- **Amazon Web Services (AWS):**
    - **Elastic Compute Cloud (EC2)**: Allows you to launch and manage virtual machines. EC2 instances can be automatically added or removed using **Auto Scaling Groups** based on traffic demand.
    - **Elastic Load Balancer (ELB)**: Automatically distributes incoming traffic across multiple EC2 instances.
    - **Elastic Container Service (ECS)** or **Elastic Kubernetes Service (EKS)**: For containerized applications, AWS allows you to scale containers easily.
- **Google Cloud Platform (GCP):**
    - **Compute Engine**: Similar to AWS EC2, GCP offers virtual machines that can be scaled up or down based on demand.

- o **Google Kubernetes Engine (GKE)**: Manages containerized applications and scales them based on usage.

- **Microsoft Azure:**
  - o **Azure Virtual Machines (VMs)**: Virtual machines that can be scaled vertically or horizontally.
  - o **Azure App Service**: PaaS offering that automatically scales web applications based on traffic.

3. Auto-Scaling Example with AWS EC2:

1. **Create an Auto Scaling Group** that defines the minimum, maximum, and desired number of EC2 instances.
2. **Configure a Scaling Policy** to add or remove instances based on traffic metrics, such as CPU utilization or request count.
   - o **Example of Auto Scaling Policy**:

```json
{
    "PolicyName": "ScaleUpPolicy",
    "AdjustmentType":
"ChangeInCapacity",
    "ScalingAdjustment": 1,
```

```
"Cooldown": 300,
"MetricAggregationType":
"Average"
}
```

- o This policy will add one instance when the CPU utilization exceeds a certain threshold.

Optimizing Database Performance for Large Data Sets

As your e-commerce store grows, your database will handle increasing amounts of data. It's essential to optimize your database to maintain fast query performance and prevent slowdowns.

1. Database Indexing

Indexing is one of the most effective ways to speed up database queries. An index allows the database to find data more efficiently by creating a data structure that speeds up the retrieval process.

- **How to Create an Index**:
  - o Index frequently queried columns, such as `product_id`, `user_id`, and `order_id`.
  - o Avoid indexing every column, as this can degrade performance.

Example:

```sql
sql
```

287

```
CREATE INDEX idx_product_name ON products
(name);
```

This index will speed up searches by product name.

2. Database Sharding

Sharding is a technique where large databases are split into smaller, more manageable pieces, called **shards**. Each shard contains a portion of the data, which can be stored on different servers. This improves query performance and reduces the load on a single server.

- **Example**: If your store has millions of users, you can shard the user data by dividing the data into several tables or databases, each containing data for a specific region or customer group.

3. Database Caching

Cache frequently accessed data, such as product details or user profiles, in memory. This reduces the need to query the database repeatedly for the same information.

- **Using Redis or Memcached** for caching:
    - Cache query results in a fast in-memory store like **Redis** or **Memcached**.

o   Set expiration times for cache data to ensure it is refreshed periodically.

Example of Using Redis for Caching:

php

```php
$redis = new Redis();
$redis->connect('127.0.0.1', 6379);

// Check if the product data is in the cache
$product_data = $redis->get('product_123');

if (!$product_data) {
    // If not in cache, fetch from the database
    $sql = "SELECT * FROM products WHERE product_id = 123";
    $result = $conn->query($sql);
    $product_data = $result->fetch_assoc();

    // Store the product data in Redis cache for 1 hour
    $redis->setex('product_123', 3600, json_encode($product_data));
}

echo $product_data;
```

4. Using Read-Replica Databases

As your database grows, read-heavy queries can put a strain on the primary database. Using **read replicas** allows you to offload read traffic to a secondary database while keeping the primary database focused on write operations.

- **AWS RDS** and **Google Cloud SQL** provide **read replicas** that can be easily set up and managed.

5. Database Query Optimization

Optimize your queries by:

- **Avoiding SELECT * queries**: Always select only the fields you need.
- **Using joins wisely**: Ensure you're not performing unnecessary joins or queries that can be optimized.
- **Using LIMIT for pagination**: When fetching large datasets, use LIMIT to return a smaller subset of data at a time.

Example of Optimizing a Query:

sql

```
-- Inefficient query
SELECT * FROM products WHERE category_id = 3;
```

```
-- Optimized query
SELECT product_id, name, price FROM products
WHERE category_id = 3 LIMIT 100;
```

6. Database Partitioning

Partitioning is the process of splitting large tables into smaller, more manageable pieces based on certain criteria (e.g., by date, category, or region). This improves query performance by narrowing down the data that needs to be processed.

- **Range Partitioning**: Partition a table by date or numeric range.
- **List Partitioning**: Partition a table by specific values (e.g., by country or region).

Conclusion

By the end of this chapter, you should have a solid understanding of how to **scale your e-commerce website** to handle increasing traffic and data. The key takeaways include:

1. **Handling High Traffic with Load Balancers**:
   o Distribute traffic across multiple servers using load balancers.
   o Use algorithms like round-robin and least connections to optimize traffic flow.
2. **Using Cloud Services to Scale Horizontally**:

291

- ○ Leverage cloud services (e.g., AWS, Google Cloud, Azure) to scale horizontally and handle growing traffic demands.
- ○ Utilize **auto-scaling** to automatically add or remove instances based on demand.

3. **Optimizing Database Performance**:

- ○ Use **database indexing, sharding, read replicas**, and **caching** to optimize performance for large datasets.
- ○ Regularly optimize queries and structure your database to improve speed and scalability.

Implementing these strategies will ensure that your e-commerce site is scalable, responsive, and capable of handling large volumes of traffic and data as your business grows.

CHAPTER 25

LEGAL CONSIDERATIONS FOR E-COMMERCE

Running an e-commerce site is not only about providing great products and a seamless user experience but also about ensuring that your website complies with legal regulations. Protecting customer data, adhering to privacy laws, and providing clear terms and conditions are essential for building trust and avoiding legal issues. In this chapter, we will cover important **legal considerations for e-commerce**, including **privacy laws and data protection regulations**, creating **terms of service, privacy policies**, and **return policies**, and implementing **cookie consent pop-ups** to ensure compliance.

Understanding Privacy Laws and Data Protection Regulations (GDPR, CCPA)

As an e-commerce business, you are collecting and processing personal data from your customers. This includes information like names, addresses, payment details, and browsing behavior. To ensure that you are handling this data ethically and legally, it is essential to understand the **privacy laws** that govern data protection.

1. General Data Protection Regulation (GDPR)

The **GDPR** is a regulation in the European Union (EU) that aims to protect the privacy and personal data of EU citizens. It applies to any business that processes personal data of EU residents, even if the business is located outside of the EU.

Key Principles of GDPR:

- **Consent**: Customers must provide clear and explicit consent for their data to be collected and processed.
- **Right to Access**: Customers have the right to request access to their personal data and how it is being used.
- **Right to Be Forgotten**: Customers can request the deletion of their personal data.
- **Data Minimization**: Collect only the data necessary for business purposes.
- **Data Security**: Implement measures to protect data from breaches or unauthorized access.

How to Comply with GDPR:

- **Obtain Consent**: Make sure you have a clear consent process when collecting personal data (e.g., through sign-up forms, checkout pages).
- **Provide Access to Data**: Allow customers to view, update, or delete their personal data upon request.

- **Data Protection**: Encrypt sensitive customer information and use secure payment gateways.

2. California Consumer Privacy Act (CCPA)

The **CCPA** is a state-level data privacy law in California that applies to businesses that collect personal data of California residents. Similar to GDPR, CCPA gives consumers control over their data and requires businesses to be transparent about how they use and share it.

Key Rights Under CCPA:

- **Right to Know**: Consumers can request information about what personal data is being collected and how it is being used.
- **Right to Delete**: Consumers can request the deletion of their personal data.
- **Right to Opt-Out**: Consumers can opt-out of the sale of their personal data.

How to Comply with CCPA:

- **Privacy Notice**: Provide a clear and accessible privacy policy that explains the data you collect and how it is used.
- **Data Requests**: Implement a process for customers to submit requests for access, deletion, and opt-out.

- **Selling Data**: If your business sells data, you need to give customers the option to opt-out and not sell their data.

3. Other Privacy Regulations:

Depending on your target market, you may need to comply with other data protection laws, such as:

- **The Children's Online Privacy Protection Act (COPPA)**: If you target children under the age of 13, COPPA imposes requirements on collecting personal data from minors.
- **The Health Insurance Portability and Accountability Act (HIPAA)**: If you handle healthcare-related information, HIPAA governs the privacy and security of medical data.

Creating Terms of Service, Privacy Policies, and Return Policies

Having well-drafted **Terms of Service**, **Privacy Policies**, and **Return Policies** is crucial for your e-commerce website. These documents protect both you and your customers, clarify the rules, and help ensure compliance with legal regulations.

1. Terms of Service (ToS)

The **Terms of Service** (also called Terms and Conditions or Terms of Use) is a legal agreement between you and your users, outlining the rules and guidelines for using your website and services. It should include the following sections:

- **Acceptance of Terms**: Clarify that users agree to the terms by using your website or purchasing from your store.
- **User Responsibilities**: Explain what is expected from users (e.g., not using the site for illegal activities).
- **Limitations of Liability**: Limit your liability in case of errors, outages, or issues with products or services.
- **Dispute Resolution**: Outline how disputes will be resolved (e.g., through arbitration or mediation).
- **Modification of Terms**: State that you can modify the terms at any time, and users will be notified.

Example of Terms of Service:

html

```
<h2>Terms of Service</h2>
<p>By using our website, you agree to the
following terms:</p>
<ul>
    <li><strong>Acceptance:</strong>        By
accessing or using our website, you agree to
these Terms of Service.</li>
    <li><strong>User Responsibilities:</strong>
You are responsible for the content you submit
```

and for maintaining the confidentiality of your account.</li>

    <li>Limitation of Liability: We are not liable for any direct, indirect, or consequential damages that may occur.</li>

    <li>Dispute Resolution: Any disputes will be resolved through arbitration in accordance with the laws of [State/Country].</li>
</ul>

2. Privacy Policy

The **Privacy Policy** explains how you collect, store, and use personal information provided by users. It is a legal requirement in many jurisdictions (such as the EU and California) and should cover the following topics:

- **Data Collection**: What personal data you collect (e.g., name, email, payment details).
- **How Data is Used**: Explain the purposes for which you use the collected data (e.g., processing orders, marketing, customer service).
- **Data Sharing**: Specify if you share data with third parties, such as payment processors, shipping providers, or marketing partners.
- **User Rights**: Outline the rights users have under privacy laws, such as access, deletion, and opting out.

- **Cookies**: Explain how you use cookies on your site and how users can manage cookie settings.

Example of a Privacy Policy:

```
html

<h2>Privacy Policy</h2>
<p>We are committed to protecting your privacy.
Here's how we handle your personal data:</p>
<ul>
    <li><strong>Data We Collect:</strong> We
collect personal information such as your name,
email address, and payment details when you make
a purchase.</li>
    <li><strong>How We Use Your Data:</strong> We
use your data to process orders, improve customer
service, and send promotional emails (with your
consent).</li>
    <li><strong>Data Sharing:</strong> We do not
share your personal data with third parties
unless it is necessary for fulfilling your order
(e.g., with payment processors or shipping
companies).</li>
    <li><strong>Your Rights:</strong> You have
the right to request access, correction, and
deletion of your personal data at any time.</li>
    <li><strong>Cookies:</strong> Our website
uses cookies to enhance your browsing experience.
```

```
You can manage your cookie preferences in your
browser settings.</li>
</ul>
```

3. Return Policy

The **Return Policy** explains the terms under which customers can return or exchange products. It builds trust with your customers by making them feel confident in their purchases.

Key elements of a return policy:

- **Return Timeframe**: Clearly state the time period during which returns are accepted (e.g., 30 days from purchase).
- **Return Eligibility**: Specify the conditions under which returns are accepted (e.g., unopened, unused items).
- **Refunds or Exchanges**: Describe whether the customer will receive a refund, exchange, or store credit.
- **Return Process**: Provide clear instructions on how customers can return products (e.g., online return form, return shipping instructions).
- **Non-Returnable Items**: Identify any products that cannot be returned (e.g., perishable goods or personalized items).

Example of a Return Policy:

```
html
```

```
<h2>Return Policy</h2>
<p>If you're not satisfied with your purchase, we
offer a 30-day return policy:</p>
<ul>
    <li><strong>Timeframe:</strong> Returns are
accepted within 30 days of purchase.</li>
    <li><strong>Condition:</strong> Items must
be   unused,   unopened,   and   in   original
packaging.</li>
    <li><strong>Refund/Exchange:</strong>    You
can choose between a full refund or exchange for
another product.</li>
    <li><strong>Return Process:</strong> Please
fill   out   our   <a   href="/returns/form">return
form</a> to initiate the return.</li>
    <li><strong>Non-Returnable   Items:</strong>
Sale items, gift cards, and personalized products
are not eligible for return.</li>
</ul>
```

Implementing Cookie Consent Pop-Ups

Many privacy laws, including GDPR, require websites to inform users about the use of cookies and to obtain their consent before setting cookies that track personal information. A **cookie consent pop-up** is a simple way to comply with these regulations.

1. Why You Need Cookie Consent:

Cookies are small pieces of data stored in the user's browser to help track sessions, improve user experience, and enable functionality like shopping carts. However, some cookies (e.g., those used for tracking or advertising) require user consent under privacy regulations like GDPR.

2. Creating a Cookie Consent Pop-Up:

- **HTML and JavaScript for Cookie Consent Pop-Up:**

  html

  ```html
  <div id="cookie-consent-banner" style="position: fixed; bottom: 0; left: 0; right: 0; background-color: #333; color: white; padding: 10px; text-align: center;">
      <p>We use cookies to improve your experience on our website. By browsing this site, you agree to our use of cookies. <a href="/privacy-policy" style="color: #ffd700;">Learn more</a></p>
      <button id="accept-cookies" style="background-color: #ffd700; padding: 5px 10px;">Accept Cookies</button>
  </div>
  ```

```
<script>
    document.getElementById('accept-
cookies').onclick = function() {
        document.getElementById('cookie-
consent-banner').style.display = 'none';

    localStorage.setItem('cookies_accepted',
'true');
    }

    if
(localStorage.getItem('cookies_accepted')
=== 'true') {
        document.getElementById('cookie-
consent-banner').style.display = 'none';
    }
</script>
```

- o This pop-up informs the user about the use of cookies and provides a button to accept them.
- o **Storage**: The user's acceptance is saved in localStorage to prevent the pop-up from appearing on subsequent visits.

Conclusion

By the end of this chapter, you should have a clear understanding of how to ensure that your e-commerce store complies with privacy laws and provides clear, transparent policies for users. Here's a summary of the key points:

1. **Privacy Laws and Data Protection**:
   o Understand and comply with regulations like **GDPR** and **CCPA** regarding customer data collection and privacy.
   o Ensure that users' personal data is handled securely and with transparency.

2. **Legal Documents**:
   o Create **Terms of Service**, **Privacy Policies**, and **Return Policies** to protect both your business and your customers.
   o Provide clear instructions for users on how their data is collected, used, and protected.

3. **Cookie Consent Pop-Ups**:
   o Implement **cookie consent pop-ups** to inform users about the use of cookies and comply with privacy laws.

These legal considerations are critical to maintaining trust with your customers, avoiding legal risks, and ensuring a smooth, compliant operation of your e-commerce store.

4o mini

CHAPTER 26

TESTING AND DEBUGGING YOUR PHP E-COMMERCE SITE

Testing and debugging are essential parts of the development process to ensure your e-commerce site works smoothly, is free of bugs, and performs optimally. This chapter will guide you through **writing test cases** using **PHPUnit, debugging common PHP and MySQL issues**, and performing **load testing** and **performance reviews** to ensure your site can handle real-world traffic and scale efficiently.

Writing Test Cases and Using PHPUnit for Testing PHP Code

PHPUnit is a popular testing framework for PHP that helps you automate the testing of your code. Writing **unit tests** ensures that each part of your codebase functions as expected and helps catch errors early in the development process.

1. What is PHPUnit?

PHPUnit is a unit testing framework that allows you to write tests for your PHP code, ensuring that individual components (functions, classes, methods) behave correctly. PHPUnit tests are

305

organized into test classes, and each test case is a method within that class.

To install PHPUnit, you can use **Composer**, which is the recommended way to manage dependencies in PHP.

1. **Install PHPUnit via Composer**:

   bash

   ```
   composer require --dev phpunit/phpunit
   ```

2. **Running PHPUnit**: Once installed, you can run PHPUnit tests using the following command:

   bash

   ```
   vendor/bin/phpunit
   ```

3. Writing Test Cases

In PHPUnit, a **test case** is a method in a test class that checks the behavior of a specific piece of code. Below is an example of a simple unit test to test the functionality of a function in your e-commerce site.

Example: Testing a Simple Function (Calculating Total Price)

Let's say you have a function that calculates the total price of an order:

php

```php
// File: src/Order.php
class Order {
    public function calculateTotal($items) {
        $total = 0;
        foreach ($items as $item) {
            $total    +=    $item['price']    *
$item['quantity'];
        }
        return $total;
    }
}
```

Now, let's write a test case to ensure that this function works as expected:

php

```php
// File: tests/OrderTest.php
use PHPUnit\Framework\TestCase;

class OrderTest extends TestCase {
    public function testCalculateTotal() {
        $order = new Order();
        $items = [
            ['price' => 100, 'quantity' => 2],
```

```
            ['price' => 50, 'quantity' => 3],
        ];
        $total = $order->calculateTotal($items);
        $this->assertEquals(350, $total);
    }
}
```

- **testCalculateTotal**: This is a test case that checks whether the `calculateTotal` function returns the correct total for the items in the order.
- **assertEquals**: This assertion checks that the calculated total matches the expected value of 350.

4. Running Tests

Once you've written your tests, you can run them by executing the following command in your terminal:

bash

```
vendor/bin/phpunit --testdox tests/OrderTest.php
```

This will run the test and output the results, helping you quickly identify whether your code is working as expected.

5. Best Practices for Writing Tests

- **Test small units of code**: Focus on testing individual methods and functions.

308

- **Use assertions**: PHPUnit provides many assertions like `assertEquals()`, `assertTrue()`, `assertFalse()`, and `assertCount()` to check if the code behaves correctly.
- **Mock dependencies**: Use mock objects or stubs to simulate complex dependencies and isolate the code you're testing.

Debugging Common Issues in PHP and MySQL

As your e-commerce site becomes more complex, you'll inevitably encounter bugs and issues. Debugging is the process of identifying, isolating, and fixing these issues. Below are common PHP and MySQL issues and how to debug them.

1. Debugging PHP Code

- **Enable Error Reporting**: Make sure you have error reporting enabled so that you can see all warnings, notices, and errors during development.

php

```php
ini_set('display_errors', 1);
error_reporting(E_ALL);
```

- o This will display all errors and warnings, which can help you identify where the issues are in your PHP code.
- **Using `var_dump()` and `print_r()`**: These functions are useful for debugging values in PHP. For instance:

```php
var_dump($variable);   // Displays the type
and value of the variable
print_r($array);           // Prints the
structure of the array
```

- **Using `Xdebug`**: **Xdebug** is a powerful debugger for PHP that integrates with IDEs like **PHPStorm** or **Visual Studio Code**. It allows you to set breakpoints, step through your code, and inspect variables.
    - o Install Xdebug and configure it in your `php.ini` file to enable remote debugging.

2. Debugging MySQL Issues

- **Enable MySQL Query Logging**: To track slow or problematic queries, enable **slow query logging** in MySQL. This helps you identify queries that take too long to execute.

```ini

```

310

```
slow_query_log = 1
slow_query_log_file                    =
/var/log/mysql/mysql-slow.log
long_query_time = 2   # Logs queries that
take longer than 2 seconds
```

- **Using EXPLAIN for Query Optimization**: When you have slow queries, use the EXPLAIN statement to analyze how MySQL executes the query and identify potential performance bottlenecks.

```sql
EXPLAIN SELECT * FROM orders WHERE
order_date > '2021-01-01';
```

This will show you how the query is executed, and whether it uses indexes efficiently.

- **Checking MySQL Logs**: MySQL logs (found in error.log or general.log) are useful for diagnosing issues related to database connections, queries, and configuration.

3. Using try-catch for Error Handling in PHP

Proper error handling is crucial for debugging and preventing crashes. Use try-catch blocks to handle exceptions gracefully.

Example:

php

```php
try {
    $conn = new mysqli($servername, $username,
$password, $dbname);
    if ($conn->connect_error) {
        throw new Exception("Connection failed:
" . $conn->connect_error);
    }
    // Database operations
} catch (Exception $e) {
    echo "Error: " . $e->getMessage();
}
```

This will catch any connection errors and display a user-friendly message.

Conducting Load Testing and Performance Reviews

As your e-commerce site grows, it's essential to test its performance under high traffic conditions. **Load testing** helps simulate real-world traffic and ensures your site can handle the load.

1. Load Testing Tools

- **Apache JMeter**: A popular open-source tool for load testing web applications. You can simulate hundreds or thousands of users and test your site's performance under different conditions.
- **LoadImpact**: A cloud-based load testing tool that allows you to test the performance of your site with real-world traffic.
- **Locust**: An open-source load testing tool written in Python. It allows you to define user behavior using Python code.

Example of Load Testing with JMeter:

1. Install JMeter on your machine.
2. Create a test plan that simulates multiple users accessing your e-commerce site.
3. Run the test and review the performance metrics such as response times, throughput, and error rates.

2. Analyzing Performance Bottlenecks

- **Server Performance**: Monitor CPU usage, memory usage, and disk I/O on your web server and database server.

- **Database Performance**: Use tools like **MySQL Workbench** to analyze slow queries and optimize them with indexing or query adjustments.
- **Caching**: Implement caching strategies (e.g., using Redis or Memcached) to speed up frequently accessed data.

3. Performance Metrics to Monitor:

- **Response Time**: The time it takes for your site to respond to a request.
- **Throughput**: The number of requests your server can handle per second.
- **Error Rate**: The percentage of failed requests.
- **Server Load**: The overall load on your server, including CPU, memory, and disk usage.

Example of Measuring Performance:

```bash
ab -n 1000 -c 50 http://your-ecommerce-site.com/
```

- This command uses **ApacheBench** (ab) to simulate 1,000 requests with 50 concurrent users to your site. It will output key performance metrics such as response time, throughput, and server load.

Conclusion

By the end of this chapter, you should have a clear understanding of how to **test and debug** your PHP-based e-commerce site effectively. The key takeaways are:

1. **Writing Test Cases**:
   - Use **PHPUnit** to automate unit tests for your PHP code.
   - Test individual functions and classes to ensure your e-commerce site runs as expected.

2. **Debugging PHP and MySQL**:
   - Enable error reporting, use debugging tools like `Xdebug`, and analyze MySQL queries with `EXPLAIN` to troubleshoot common issues.
   - Handle errors gracefully using `try-catch` blocks.

3. **Load Testing and Performance Reviews**:
   - Use tools like **JMeter** or **Locust** for load testing to simulate high traffic and identify performance bottlenecks.
   - Optimize server and database performance through query optimization, caching, and monitoring resource usage.

With these testing and debugging strategies, you can ensure that your e-commerce site is not only functional but also performs optimally under high traffic conditions.

CHAPTER 27

LAUNCHING AND MAINTAINING YOUR E-COMMERCE STORE

Launching an e-commerce store is a huge milestone in your business journey, but the work doesn't stop there. Once your store is live, continuous maintenance and monitoring are essential to ensure it stays secure, performs well, and meets your customers' needs. This chapter will guide you through the process of **preparing your site for launch, setting up backups and monitoring for uptime**, and **maintaining and updating your store post-launch**.

Preparing Your Site for Launch

Before your e-commerce store goes live, you need to ensure that everything is functioning as expected. A successful launch depends on careful preparation to avoid common issues such as broken links, slow performance, or security vulnerabilities.

1. Final Testing and Quality Assurance (QA)

Before launching, perform a thorough round of testing and **quality assurance (QA)** to ensure that everything on the site works as expected. Key areas to focus on include:

317

- **Functionality Testing**: Ensure that all features, such as product search, checkout, login, and payment processing, work correctly.

- **Cross-Browser and Device Testing**: Test your site on various browsers (Chrome, Firefox, Safari, Edge) and devices (desktop, tablet, mobile) to ensure it works seamlessly across different platforms.

- **Usability Testing**: Ensure the site is easy to navigate and that customers can find what they're looking for quickly.

- **Security Testing**: Check for vulnerabilities in your site. Ensure that HTTPS is enabled, passwords are hashed, and personal data is protected.

Checklist for Pre-Launch Testing:

- Ensure all **links are functional**.
- Test the **checkout process** and payment gateways (using sandbox/test modes if available).
- Verify that the **contact form** and other communication channels are working.
- Check that the site is **responsive** (works well on mobile devices and desktops).
- Confirm **SEO settings** are correct, including metadata, sitemap, and robots.txt files.

2. Optimize Your Site for Performance

Before launch, make sure your site is optimized for speed and performance. A slow-loading website can frustrate customers and harm SEO rankings.

- **Image Optimization**: Compress images to reduce load times without compromising quality.
- **Minify CSS and JavaScript**: Reduce file sizes by removing unnecessary spaces and comments from CSS and JavaScript files.
- **Enable Caching**: Ensure caching mechanisms (like browser caching and server-side caching) are set up.

3. Set Up Analytics and Tracking

Set up **Google Analytics** or another analytics tool to track visitor activity on your site. Monitoring key metrics like **traffic, bounce rate, conversion rate**, and **average order value** will help you assess your store's performance and identify areas for improvement.

- **Set up Google Tag Manager** to easily manage and deploy tracking scripts for things like **Google Analytics, Facebook Pixel**, and **conversion tracking**.
- **Configure Goals and E-commerce Tracking** in Google Analytics to measure key actions such as product views, add-to-carts, and completed purchases.

4. Prepare for Customer Support:

Make sure your customer support systems are ready. This includes:

- Setting up your **help desk** or **support ticket system** (e.g., Zendesk, Freshdesk).
- Adding **live chat** functionality (e.g., using Intercom or Tawk.to).
- Ensuring your **FAQ section** is populated with answers to common questions.
- Provide clear contact details (email, phone number) and return policy.

Setting Up Backups and Monitoring for Uptime

Once your store is live, ensuring its reliability and safety is paramount. **Backing up your data** and **monitoring uptime** will help you maintain your site's stability and recover from any issues that arise.

1. Setting Up Backups

Data loss or a website crash can happen at any time, so it's critical to set up regular backups of your site and its data.

- **File Backups**: Backup all files, including images, CSS, JavaScript, and PHP files. This can be done manually, but it's more efficient to automate the process.
- **Database Backups**: Regularly back up your MySQL database, which contains product information, customer data, orders, and other essential details.

Automating Backups:

- Use tools like **UpdraftPlus** (for WordPress) or **JetBackup** (for cPanel) to schedule automated backups.
- Store backups in multiple locations, such as cloud storage (e.g., AWS S3, Google Drive, or Dropbox), to ensure redundancy.
- Create **backup retention policies** to keep multiple versions of your backups, allowing you to restore from a specific point in time.

Example of Scheduling MySQL Backups: You can set up automated MySQL backups using **cron jobs** on a Linux server.

```bash
0 3 * * * mysqldump -u username -p'password'
database_name > /path/to/backup/folder/backup-
$(date +\%F).sql
```

This will back up the database daily at 3 AM.

2. Monitoring Website Uptime

Website uptime is critical to ensuring your store is always available to customers. Use uptime monitoring tools to receive notifications if your website goes down.

- **Uptime Monitoring Services**: Tools like **UptimeRobot, Pingdom,** and **StatusCake** can monitor your website's uptime in real time. They will alert you via email or SMS if your site goes down, enabling you to take quick action.
- **Set Up Alerts**: Ensure that you're receiving alerts for issues like server downtime, slow page load times, or server errors (e.g., 500 internal server errors).

3. Server Monitoring:

Use tools like **New Relic** or **Datadog** to monitor server performance in real-time. These tools help track key metrics such as CPU usage, memory usage, and response times, allowing you to identify performance bottlenecks before they become problems.

Maintaining and Updating Your Store Post-Launch

After your e-commerce store is launched, ongoing maintenance is crucial for keeping your site secure, updated, and running smoothly.

1. Regular Software Updates

Regularly update your e-commerce platform, themes, plugins, and any third-party services you use. Keeping software up-to-date ensures that security vulnerabilities are patched and that you have access to the latest features.

- **Security Patches**: Ensure that all security patches are applied promptly. Vulnerabilities in your platform, plugins, or server software can be exploited by attackers if not patched.
- **Updates for Performance**: Update your software to access optimizations that improve site speed and performance.

2. Security Audits

Regularly conduct security audits to identify potential weaknesses in your site. This includes:

- **Monitoring for Suspicious Activity**: Use security plugins or services like **Sucuri** to monitor for malware or unauthorized access attempts.
- **SSL Certificates**: Ensure your SSL certificates are up to date to maintain secure connections with customers.
- **Login Protection**: Implement two-factor authentication (2FA) for admin users and monitor failed login attempts.

3. Customer Feedback and Reviews

Keep track of customer feedback and reviews to identify pain points or areas for improvement. This helps you provide better customer service and makes it easier to fine-tune your store.

- **Use Customer Feedback**: Set up surveys or ask for feedback on your product pages to get direct insights from users.
- **Monitor Product Reviews**: Actively monitor reviews and respond to customer complaints or queries to show that you care about their satisfaction.

4. Adding New Features and Content

As your business evolves, you will likely need to add new features or content to your store.

- **New Products**: Regularly update your product catalog with new items, product descriptions, and high-quality images.
- **Seasonal Promotions**: Run seasonal promotions, sales, and discounts to keep customers engaged and boost sales.
- **SEO and Content Updates**: Keep your SEO strategy fresh by updating content and optimizing product pages for better search engine rankings.

5. Analyzing Performance Metrics

Use your analytics and monitoring tools to regularly analyze key performance indicators (KPIs). This includes tracking metrics like traffic, conversion rates, and average order value (AOV).

- **A/B Testing**: Perform **A/B testing** to test different layouts, product pages, or offers to see which performs better with your audience.
- **Conversion Rate Optimization (CRO)**: Regularly review your checkout process, product pages, and site design to optimize the flow and increase conversions.

Conclusion

Launching an e-commerce store is just the beginning; ongoing maintenance, security, and optimization are necessary to ensure its continued success. By preparing your site for launch, setting up **backups and uptime monitoring**, and maintaining and updating your store regularly, you can keep your e-commerce business running smoothly and provide an excellent customer experience. Here are the key takeaways:

1. **Preparing for Launch**: Test your site thoroughly, optimize performance, and set up analytics.
2. **Backups and Monitoring**: Implement automated backups and monitor uptime and server performance to ensure your site stays reliable.

3. **Post-Launch Maintenance**: Regularly update software, perform security audits, listen to customer feedback, and optimize site performance to keep your store running at its best.

With these practices in place, your e-commerce store will be well-positioned for success, offering a smooth and secure experience for your customers while remaining adaptable to growth and changing market conditions.

www.ingramcontent.com/pod-product-compliance
Lightning Source LLC
LaVergne TN
LVHW022334060326
832902LV00022B/4034